S0-BOM-861

ISBN 0-439-75377-5

51599>

EAN

9 780439 753777

SCHOLASTIC

Writing Lessons
for the Content Areas

Standards-Based Lessons That Help Students Plan, Organize, and Draft Their Nonfiction Writing in Social Studies and Science

Includes lessons on

* **Using graphic organizers**

* **Note taking and summarizing**

* **Learning specialized vocabulary**

* **Analyzing information**

INCLUDES A
COMPLETE
INTEGRATED

Cheryl M. Sigmon and Sylvia M. Ford

SCHOLASTIC

Writing Lessons for the Content Areas

Standards-Based Lessons That Help Students Plan, Organize, and
Draft Their Nonfiction Writing in Social Studies and Science

Cheryl M. Sigmon

Sylvia M. Ford

New York • Toronto • London • Auckland • Sydney
Mexico City • New Delhi • Hong Kong • Buenos Aires

Teaching *Resources*

DEDICATION

We owe a debt of gratitude to two people without whom this book would not have come to fruition. Executive editor Joanna Davis-Swing re-envisioned the original manuscript and devoted a great deal of time and energy toward this creation. Development and project editor, Merryl Maleska Wilbur showed endless patience, gentle guidance, a vision for what would make this book unique, and the greatest level of professionalism, even when "the going got tough." Joanna and Merryl both share a sincere dedication to the teaching profession, which is what this book and our series of writing books are all about. In the truest sense, this book would not be without these two great women. Our heartfelt thanks to them!

CMS and SMF

To all of my former teachers, principals, and co-workers who inspired my passion for literacy.

SMF

To my husband, Don, and my daughters, Melissa and Susan, for their constant support.

SMF

To Ray for always being there for me, even when I'm writing for endless hours . . .

CMS

ACKNOWLEDGEMENTS

Tammy Bates, Sand Creek Elementary School, North Vernon, Indiana

Lara Crowley and Debbie Panchisin, Curriculum Consultants, Appoquinimink School District, Odessa, Delaware

Joy Dewing and Leslie Lewis, Central Middle School, Kokomo, Indiana

Lisa Gilpin, Sand Creek Elementary School, North Vernon, Indiana

Gayle Hinton, Coordinator of Science, Social Studies and Health, Lexington School District Two, West Columbia, South Carolina

Ann Hollar, Horace Mann Elementary School, Huntington, Indiana

Kokomo-Center Township Consolidated School Corporation, Kokomo, Indiana

Kay Kinder, Coordinator of Instructional Services

Middle Schools: Bon Air, Cindy Dwyer, Principal; Central, Brian VanBuskirk, Principal;

Elementary Schools: Columbian, Sharon Hahn, Principal; Darrough Chapel, Paula Concus, Principal; Pettit Park, Claudette Renfro, Principal; Washington, Linda Campbell, Principal

Richland School District One, Columbia, South Carolina

Linda Gillespie and Deborah Green-Wilson, Title One Office

Richard Moore, Principal, and Nan Gray, Curriculum Resource Teacher, Logan Elementary

Delores Gilliard, Principal, and Kitty Faden, Curriculum Resource Teacher, Greenview Elementary School

Tony Ross, Principal, and Sally Mills, 6th District Elementary School, Covington, Kentucky

Todd Leininger and upper grade teachers at North Miami Elementary School, Denver, Indiana

Cover design by Jason Robinson.
Interior design by Solutions by Design, Inc.
Photos courtesy of the authors.

ISBN: 0-439-75377-5

1 2 3 4 5 6 7 8 9 10   40   12 11 10 09 08 07 06 05

Table of Contents

INTRODUCTION 5

The Power of Writing 5

Writing in the Content Areas: Two Purposes That Work Together 5

What We Focus On in This Book and Why 6

    Specialized Vocabulary 6

    Graphic/Visual Organizers 6

    Text Patterns and Text Structure 7

    Research Skills 7

    Writing for Authentic Purposes 7

How the Skills Focuses and Standards Apply to the Lessons 7

Coming to America: Ellis Island—A Model Unit of Integrated Instruction 8

The Mini-Lessons

    The Framework for These Mini-Lessons 8

    Pragmatics and Purposes of the Daily Mini-Lesson 8

Beyond This Book 9

Language Arts Standards Index 10

Mini-Lessons

SECTION ONE: Retaining and Enriching Specialized Vocabulary 12

    Section Introduction 12

    Key terms: the ABCs of specialized vocabulary 14

    Writing a glossary 16

    Learning word associations through concept circles 17

    Exploring the structure of specialized vocabulary words 18

    Working with words through poetry: haiku 20

    Working with words through poetry: acrostic poems 22

SECTION TWO: Using Graphic/Visual Organizers 23

    Section Introduction 23

    Paragraph planners—paragraphs that compare and contrast information 25

    Paragraph planners—main ideas and supporting details 27

    Pro/con t-charts 28

    5W's graphic organizer 29

    Persuasive writing flow chart 31

SECTION THREE: Textual Organizers and Nonfiction Text Patterns 33

Section Introduction 33

Organizing by Q and A 35

Using expository terms to organize text 37

Using narrative story structure with expository material 39

Selecting an appropriate text pattern 41

Three-Part Lesson: Writing a Well-Structured Expository Composition 43

Part 1: Creating a main idea/details outline 43

Part 2: Using transitions to connect ideas 45

Part 3: Writing the composition 46

SECTION FOUR: Putting Research Skills to Work 47

Section Introduction 47

Developing open-ended questions 49

Two-Part Lesson: Organizing Information for Writing 50

Part 1: Using a research organizer for taking notes 50

Completed research organizer 51

Part 2: Writing a summary from organized notes 52

Narrowing a research topic using a table of contents 53

Summarizing 55

Making scientific observations 57

SECTION FIVE: Writing for Authentic Purposes 59

Section Introduction 59

Filling out job applications 61

Publishing on a web page 62

Writing persuasive letters 64

Writing editorials 67

Three-Part Lesson: Writing and Giving a Speech 69

Part 1: Planning and organizing 69

Parts 2 and 3: Writing and giving the speech 71

Writing a nonfiction book review 72

Coming to America: Ellis Island—A Model Unit of Integrated Instruction 74

APPENDICES 90

Alpha-Key Words Chart 90

5 W's Organizer 91

Persuasive Writing Flow Chart 92

Research Organizer 93

Job Application 94

Research Report Organizer (One Source) 95

BIBLIOGRAPHY 96

Introduction

The Power of Writing

The power of writing in the classroom has become increasingly indisputable during the past two decades. Most educators are convinced that writing is an effective method for teaching children how to read. Lucy Calkins, a trailblazing researcher in the area of writing and literacy, once said, "Writing is reading from the inside out." What a perfect way to sum up that closest of connections between these two areas of the language arts!

We also see that writing allows students to transfer much of what they have learned. As students create their own stories, we see the evidence of their having heard and read well-crafted stories from their earliest years. Here, finding voice within their own writing, is a rich history of exposure to literature. Characters, plots, and settings that made impressions on them as listeners and readers now re-emerge in new and original forms. We see their transfer of word knowledge in spelling, word patterns, and vocabulary choices. Subsequently, students' writing guides our instruction as we discover the need to teach more or to teach differently, according to what our students have written. Yes, writing has become powerful to both teachers and writers.

As if the reading-writing connection were not enough reason to convince us that classroom writing time and instruction is essential, there is also strong evidence that writing may be one of the best tools available for enhancing thinking and learning in general. Writing expert Donald Murray sums it up this way:

> "Writing is thinking. Writing, in fact, is the most disciplined form of thinking. It allows us to be precise, to stand back and examine what we have thought, to see what our words really mean, to see if they stand up to our own critical eye, make sense, will be understood by someone else." (Murray, 1984)

Writing in the Content Areas: Two Purposes That Work Together

Researchers of best practice instruction consider writing to be an effective tool *in all subject areas* for activating prior knowledge, eliciting questions that draw students into the subject, building comprehension, teaching vocabulary, promoting discussion, and reviewing and reflecting on ideas already covered (Zemelman, et.al., 1998). In many high-functioning classrooms, an observer would find it impossible to separate language arts and content area instruction, as those disciplines can so successfully and naturally be woven together. In our opinion, this integration simulates real-world tasks: Rarely does a task, whether personal or work-related, involve only reading or writing or knowledge of particular content. Usually a task requires a blend of these skills and knowledge.

As another important benefit, the integration of instruction in language arts with that of content areas helps teachers deal successfully with the pressure of time constraints in the classroom. Integration of curriculum has surfaced as a way to manage the myriad standards that are presently crammed into the limited time frame provided for instruction. If, for example, the language arts curriculum says that students must be able to write a persuasive composition, why not teach that skill in the context of exploring the destruction of endangered habitats during a science lesson or as students form opinions about the creation of debt in American economics? If the language arts curriculum states that students must learn to write poetry, why not teach poetry along with specialized vocabulary about asteroids, comets, and magnetars in a science class? The language skills of reading, writing, speaking, and listening beg for a context that is so easily, richly, and plentifully provided through the subject areas that we teach daily in our classrooms.

Teaching writing simultaneously with content material can achieve an even greater purpose. A mainstay method of teaching and learning in traditional classrooms has been the required memorization of facts and figures. However, in a quickly changing world where even something as standard as a globe can seem obsolete, our instructional efforts need to be refocused. It is increasingly imperative that students learn how to acquire the information they need, how to manage that information, and how to communicate it effectively to others. Through this effective application of language skills, students truly can gain power in their lives today and beyond.

What We Focus On in This Book and Why

This book provides instruction for essential elements and tools that will help students write more effectively and that are particularly important for the intermediate grades. These elements and tools are connected to content area instruction in which we demonstrate how both writing and content curriculums can be taught simultaneously. In the lessons, we model for you how manageable it is to combine instruction in both areas and how science, social studies, history, health, and other subject areas provide appropriate contexts for your writing lessons.

So, what *are* the writing tools you'll find in this book that apply so easily to the content areas you're teaching? Below we give an overview of the toolbox with its five unique types of tools.

Specialized Vocabulary

The tools in this section not only help students comprehend content concepts but also help them to communicate these major ideas and concepts. Using the vocabulary germane to the subjects they're studying, students have the opportunity to develop a familiarity with these terms and to describe and demonstrate their new understandings. The lessons in this section offer numerous ways to help students grasp deeper meanings of the content area words they encounter. Students work with specialized vocabulary as they write original poems—haikus and acrostic poems—and also as they categorize, define, and analyze content words through concept maps, student-created glossaries, and word webs.

Graphic/Visual Organizers

Many students find that they can better organize their writing and more clearly present their ideas if they can call on visual aids from their writing toolbox. In this section, we demonstrate how to use graphic organizers to reach these students—students for whom the visual mode is the primary way of learning. Well-constructed visual aids help them to compare and contrast two, three, or more concepts; to plan out stronger paragraphs (affording them a glimpse of the infrastructure of the paragraph); to form reasoned opinions based on a sorting out of facts; and to visualize the flow of different kinds of writing such as news articles and persuasive letters.

Text Patterns and Text Structure

This section demonstrates how various text organizers and patterns become tools that transfer from the student as a reader to the student as a writer. With these tools, students can utilize the external and internal arrangements of expository text in two ways: As readers they can better grasp ideas, and as writers they can better frame their discussions. The mini-lessons in this section immerse students in several different types of internal structures used in expository writing—for instance, the question and answer format and the main idea and supporting details structure. In addition, one lesson invites students to apply narrative structure to writing about content facts while another teaches them to look for and make use of certain terms as clues to expository text structure and message.

Research Skills

This section provides students with tools for doing research in a manner that helps them explore, examine, and organize the many different kinds of information that are available today. These mini-lessons present techniques for effective questioning, note-taking, summarizing of key concepts and ideas, and recording accurate scientific observations, while tapping into natural curiosity to guide research. The tools in these mini-lessons take the dread out of research!

Writing for Authentic Purposes

The tools in this section are somewhat like carrots that can be dangled to encourage and motivate even reluctant writers. To a certain extent, all students write to please themselves—they'll write to please you, but they'll write with passion when they have a real purpose and audience. These lessons help them do everything from exploring careers in specific content areas to filling out job applications, from writing editorials to creating Web sites. We don't want them to ask, "Why are we learning this?" We want them to see the application and the true power of writing through real purposes.

How the Skills Focuses and Standards Apply to the Lessons

Beyond merely integrating instruction in this book, we also want to offer the means necessary for you to achieve a balance so that both the language arts area and the content area receive appropriate emphasis. In these lessons, we weave together instruction so that students can practice and refine their language skills while learning and applying new content information.

In terms of skills and standards, however, our focus is language arts. The Skills Focus feature of each mini-lesson lists the specific language arts standards addressed by that lesson. The highlighted content area is intended simply to illustrate how integration can occur within subject areas and is not limited to the specific content depicted in the lesson. (Be assured, however, that we did research the science and social studies standards of many states to arrive at an appropriate context for grades 4–6.)

We encourage you to blend your own content area curriculum with the specified language arts standards to arrive at a relevant and appropriate lesson for your particular students. For example, the arctic tern is the subject of our haiku lesson. Teaching students about haiku in your classroom might coincide with your study of exploration of the New World or perhaps with a science unit on the universe. Our lesson on text organization through questions and answers using the science principles of animal adaptation could also be applied to your study of force and matter. So, we hope that you'll look beyond the content that we've chosen in our lessons to see clearly the application to whatever the curriculum might be in your classroom.

Coming to America: Ellis Island—A Model Unit of Integrated Instruction

As mentioned above, most of the lessons in this book are one- and two-day mini-lessons that present different tools for expository writing and demonstrate how integrated curriculum works. These lessons can be used with almost any content in any discipline. In order to offer an illustration of a more extended and complete integrated lesson, however, we include one that spans several weeks and that thoroughly integrates language arts standards and goals with specific content standards and goals: *Coming to America: Ellis Island,* pages 74–89.

The context for this integrated unit is civics, within an intermediate-grades social studies curriculum. Through such benchmark questions as, "What does it mean to be a United States citizen?"; "What is citizenship?"; and "How does a person become a citizen?" this unit explores the topic "The Role of Citizens." Within this unit, which extends over a period of approximately 12 days, we offer a window into the thorough integration of social studies and language arts skills, specifically writing skills. Among many other skills, the writing mini-lessons highlight the teaching of conventions of punctuation and grammar, applying graphic organizers for planning, and conducting interviews prior to writing.

Some important research supports this unit's approach. The unit grows out of a powerful environmental method of writing instruction (Hillocks, 1986) in which process and procedures are taught together, which encourages collaboration among writers, and which builds in more student-directed criteria and accountabilities. You'll notice the many checklists that help to establish these criteria. In grades 4–`6, we're moving students toward independence as writers, and in this unit, you'll see how we suggest accomplishing this.

The Mini-Lessons

The Framework for These Mini-Lessons

Our many combined years of classroom experience have led us to realize that we must make the most of powerful sound bites during instructional time. Although we may be able to keep students in desks and may even be able to keep their heads turned in our direction, we know that keeping their undivided attention riveted on our lesson for longer than say 15 minutes is next to impossible. The instructions for each mini-lesson in this book are packed tightly into about a 10- to 15-minute time frame for that very reason.

Whether you choose to bring science or social studies into your writing time or writing into your science and social studies time, we suggest adopting a workshop approach for these lessons. The workshop framework for our lessons is traditionally divided into three parts: 1) the teacher's model lesson and direct instruction; 2) the students' writing and application time; and 3) time for students to share what they've been working on. This book deals with the first portion of time, the model lesson, although lessons certainly have an impact on students' writing and application time and on the sharing time. During the first part of the lesson, the teacher will write and offer direct instruction daily. Modeling may be done in any number of ways but generally includes the teacher sitting down to write while the students observe. Because this serves as the teacher's direct, explicit instruction, it may not be as interactive as instruction during other parts of the day.

Pragmatics and Purposes of the Daily Mini-Lesson

Our favorite way to model the daily writing is to sit down beside an overhead projector, simulating as closely as possible the posture the students will assume as they write. We face the class, allowing the students to watch and listen as we make the decisions that writers make when they compose.

For each lesson, we include a brief list of materials and resources particular to that lesson's activity. These specific items are intended to augment a standard set of materials and resources that apply to most of the mini-lessons in this book. These daily materials may include transparencies with lines similar to the lined paper students will use; plastic sheets in which you insert your lined transparencies; and transparency pens in multicolors.

If you don't have access to an overhead projector, you can model writing on chart paper or on a chalk- or dry-erase board (though this last option won't allow you to save your compositions). You'll still need pens or chalk in a variety of colors. In the upper grades, composing on a chalkboard or chart becomes more cumbersome as the pieces are longer and as they are often used over multiple days.

Teachers should view the 10- to 15-minute model lessons as serving several purposes, all of which are important:

When a teacher uses a transparency to model writing, he or she can face the class and allow students to watch and listen to the decision-making and composing processes.

☆ To model how writers get their ideas

☆ To model the basic conventions of writing

☆ To model good writing habits

☆ To model the writing process

☆ To offer writing options to students

☆ To model the application of writing skills to the content being taught

☆ To encourage students to think

☆ To motivate students to write

If you are a teacher who hasn't yet had experience with mini-lessons, remember the words of writing guru Nancie Atwell: "We only have to write a little better than they do for them to take away something from our demonstrations." So, take a deep breath and try it. Day by day the modeling becomes easier and you'll quickly see how your students grow because of this experience.

Beyond This Book

Although it is not intended to provide a comprehensive curriculum, the toolbox of practical ideas that you will find in this book can be used independently as a lesson source or as a supplement to our series of books, *Just-Right Writing Mini-Lessons* for Grade 1 (Scholastic, 2004), Grades 2–3 (Scholastic, 2005), and Grades 4–6 (Scholastic, in press). In those books, we do provide a complete instructional guide for a writing curriculum based on the writing standards in several states and using both fiction and nonfiction of different varieties. Those lessons focus primarily on the mini-lesson portion of the Writing Workshop for a language arts class.

Our most sincere hope for this book is that through its use you'll see just how easily you can deliver writing and content instruction. Ultimately, we hope that through the integration of curriculum, the writing tools provided, and the natural context of the lessons, your students will be successful in their daily lessons and in the transfer of what they learn to their roles in the real world as powerful writers.

LANGUAGE ARTS STANDARDS INDEX

NOTE: You can use this index in two different ways. First, you can reference specific mini-lessons that allow you to teach standards pertinent to your own curriculum and instructional needs. You can also use the index to determine the phase of the writing process within which a particular standard or lesson is most appropriately taught. As you can see from the number of lessons relating to the standard, most lessons offer numerous opportunities to reteach and reinforce your instruction of these skills and strategies.

STANDARDS BY PHASE	LESSON PAGE NUMBER
Planning for Writing: The Pre-Writing Stage	
Generate ideas for stories and descriptions in pictures and books, magazines, textbooks, the Internet, in conversation with others, and in newspapers, and through brainstorming	53, 67, 75, 83
Plan writing with details, using lists, graphic organizers, notes and logs, outlines, conceptual maps, learning logs, and timelines	14, 17, 25, 27, 28, 29, 31, 41, 43, 50, 52, 67, 69, 76, 78, 79, 80, 83, 87
Organize writing into a logical order: Select an organized structure/form that best suits purpose: chronological order, cause and effect, similarity and differences, pose and answer questions, climactic order, and general to specific; Choose point of view based on purpose, audience, length and format requirements	16, 25, 28, 29, 31, 35, 37, 39, 41, 50, 52, 55, 61, 76, 85
Take notes from authoritative sources (i.e. almanacs, newspapers, periodicals and the Internet) by identifying main ideas, evaluating relevancy, and paraphrasing information in resource materials	14, 50, 57, 64, 69, 71, 76, 77
Locate information by using prefaces, appendixes, citations, endnotes, and bibliographic references	50, 77
Frame questions to direct research and raise new questions for further investigation	49, 57, 75, 76
Writing the Draft	
Use resources for spelling: Use correct spelling for frequently used words (including irregular words, compound words, and homophones) and common word patterns; Use classroom resources for spelling (dictionary, thesaurus, Spell Check)	18
Write effective beginning, middle, and end (including well-developed character, setting, and plot)	29, 39, 78, 79
Write pieces with multiple paragraphs: Include an introductory paragraph with central idea and topic sentence; Include supporting paragraphs with appropriate facts, details, explanations, or concrete examples; Use appropriate transitions to link paragraphs; Write a concluding paragraph that summarizes points	78, 79, 80, 81, 83, 84, 85
Making Writing Cleaner and Clearer (Conventions)	
Conjunctions: Use conjunctions to connect ideas and avoid excessive use	45, 46
Interjections: Use interjections to make writing expressive	84
Commas: Use commas with appositives; Use after introductory phrases and clauses	81, 83, 86
Quotation Marks: Use in conversation; in titles (articles, poems, songs, short stories, chapters)	80, 83
Apostrophes: Use with singular and plural possessives	85
Hyphens and Ellipsis Points: Use hyphens to divide words; Use ellipsis to show omissions in text	81, 83

STANDARDS BY PHASE	LESSON PAGE NUMBER
Making Writing Better (Revisions)	
Form imagery: Use figures of speech; Use sensory details, and/or concrete examples	79, 83
Use transitions to connect ideas	45, 46
Revise writing to improve word choice and precision of vocabulary: Use adjectives and adverbs to make writing more vivid and/or precise	22
Make word choices appropriate to audience and purpose, including the use of specialized vocabulary	14, 16, 17, 18, 20, 22, 61
Analyze published examples as models for writing	16, 69
Revise writing for meaning, clarity, and focus: Add and delete; Combine and rearrange words, sentences, and paragraphs; Use modifiers, coordination, and subordination to expand and embed ideas	81, 82, 83, 85, 87
Writing in a Variety of Forms	
Write narratives that describe and explain familiar objects, events, and experiences: Use a range of narrative devices, i.e.: dialogue or suspense; Use literary conflict, elements, and devices	39, 85
Write in response to what is read and written	20, 41, 43, 45, 46, 49, 55, 84, 85
Write informational pieces, summarizing and organizing ideas gained from multiple sources in useful ways, including charts, graphs, outlines, and lists	17, 27, 49, 52, 57, 62, 75, 77, 87
Write summaries of reading selections to include main ideas and significant details	27, 37, 55
Write a friendly letter	84
Write persuasive pieces: Support with relevant evidence and effective emotional appeals; Follow simple organizational pattern with most appealing statements first, address reader concerns; Write persuasive pieces for different purposes	28, 61, 64, 67, 71, 72
Write patterned, rhymed, unrhymed, and free verse poems	20, 22
Write in learning logs and journals to discover, develop and refine ideas including other curricular areas	57, 84
Write plays	87, 88, 89
Publishing and Polishing Our Writing	
Edit for correctness, meaning, and clarity: Use appropriate references when editing—including dictionary, books, and simple thesaurus	82
Use a simple checklist for revising and editing, working independently and collaboratively	82, 87
Use organizational features of text (page numbering, alphabetizing, glossaries, chapter heading, tables of contents, indexes, and captions)	16, 53
Respond in constructive ways to others' writings	82
Use word processing and available technology for presentation	87
Share writing orally with others	71
Publish in various formats	62, 72, 87

Retaining and Enriching Specialized Vocabulary

V ocabulary instruction is a common thread throughout the curriculum of all language arts and content areas. As educators, we aim to have our students learn the meanings of new words because we know that their assimilation of these words will deepen their understanding of texts and concepts. As stated in *The Report of the National Reading Panel* (2000), "The importance of vocabulary knowledge has long been recognized in the development of reading skills. As early as 1924, researchers noted that growth in reading power relies on continuous growth in word knowledge."

Even without benefit of the preponderance of research on the subject, few teachers would dispute the obvious connection between vocabulary and achievement. Further, because the majority of reading and writing both in the "real world" and in the "testing world" is connected to informational rather than narrative text, we understand how essential it is to facilitate students' acquisition of the specialized vocabulary that will help them succeed with content area literacy. However, vocabulary instruction in the content areas presents a particular challenge to teachers for two main reasons: 1) The content is generally laden with more unfamiliar words than, say, literature selections are; and 2) the stakes are higher because the unfamiliar words in informational selections have a greater direct impact on comprehension than do unfamiliar words in narrative text (Pikulski and Templeton, 2004).

So, with all this in mind, the critical question remains: How can we best help our students develop word knowledge in the content area arena? With limited time, how can we focus on vocabulary in a way that will make a significant impact on student achievement?

Let's take a look first at what won't accomplish our goal. Both research and classroom experience have demonstrated for many years now that relying on mere repetition and memorization to teach vocabulary doesn't work. Instead, students will learn words because of meaningful associations (Stahl and Fairbanks, 1986). Students must be engaged in words in ways that allow them to build a schema of meaning and relationships to help them process the words. As *The Report of the National Reading Panel* states, "Vocabulary learning is effective when it entails active engagement in learning tasks."

Taking all these points into consideration, we have concluded that one of the most effective ways to engage students in vocabulary acquisition is through writing. And, if specialized vocabulary is essential for achievement, why not teach this through writing in the content areas? The mini-lessons in this section address this goal directly: They engage students in the use, application, and practice of new words in different ways for different purposes.

Several of this section's lessons help students in their exploration of a word's definition and its connections to the meanings of related words. For example, students are asked in one lesson not only to use, but also to create their own glossary, and in another lesson to categorize terms by shared concepts. One of the lessons asks students to engage in a compass vocabulary activity that enables them to examine word roots and affixes, thus analyzing the structure of words. This is a key skill in working with specialized terminology because many expository terms are built from related roots (think of how many scientific words have the prefix *photo-* or the suffix *–metric,* for example).

A number of other lessons guide students to experiment with words as they experience and write poetry, ranging from haiku to free verse. Within the creative context of writing poetry, students learn to work with specific content terms that communicate just the right meaning.

Knowing what the research says and considering what we must teach in the confines of a busy classroom day, our overall goals for vocabulary instruction, as embodied in this book's mini-lessons, are as follows:

☆ Reduce the number of vocabulary words to be taught directly both in language arts and in the content areas. Ask yourself two questions to achieve this: Is the word critical to understanding the text? Is this word useful for my students to know in their further reading and writing? If the word passes both tests, find a way to get students actively involved in the word.

☆ Teach strategies for vocabulary acquisition to enable students to figure out the words. Identifying meaningful word parts and drawing relationships between and among words will serve students well in gaining independence and will get them to utilize their higher-order cognitive skills.

☆ Integrate instruction into a rich context as much as possible, bringing content vocabulary into language arts instruction and language arts instruction into your content area. This will lend relevance to your instruction and will be a tremendous time-saver.

☆ Use writing to engage students actively in learning new words.

When students become so familiar with a word that not only is its meaning known, but it also becomes a comfortable "friend," they will not be afraid to use that word in informed and exciting new ways. At the same time, their grasp of content concepts will deepen remarkably. We hope you'll find that these lessons help your students begin to accomplish just such goals!

Key terms: the ABCs of specialized vocabulary

EXPLANATION: In addition to helping students enhance their vocabulary knowledge, this lesson can be used to sharpen reading and listening skills. The writing component, summarizing, will also help students to focus on what they have read or heard in an easy, concise way as they practice using germane vocabulary.

Skills Focus

Planning writing with details
Taking notes from authoritative sources
Making appropriate word choices
Evaluating relevancy
. . . as part of the study of earth science

Materials & Resources

☆ Transparency of Alpha-Key Words chart (see Appendix, p. 90)
☆ Photocopies, one for each student, of Alpha-Key Words chart

Quick Hints

The Alpha-Key Words chart can also be used as a springboard for class discussions after students have read or listened to information in any content area.

STEPS

1. Explain to students that to become better, more efficient readers and writers of informational material, they need to be able to locate, understand, and utilize key words and phrases. These terms convey the most important concepts in a piece of content area writing; without them, students can miss the heart of the matter. Point out that often publishers of nonfiction texts use special effects—such as highlighting, italics, and underlining—to call attention to these words. In addition, these words may be emphasized through repetition or stated in the heading.

2. Call students' attention to a section of content material they are currently studying. For this lesson, we use a chapter from an earth science textbook.

3. Using a transparency, present the Alpha-Key Words chart (Appendix, p. 90) to the class. Read through a page or so to demonstrate how you list the key words or phrases you find as you read. Stress to students that you're listing only key words or phrases on the chart, and that it's not a goal to find a word for each letter of the alphabet. Below is a sample chart, based on a science textbook chapter about Earth's atmosphere:

A	B	C	D	E	F
atmosphere air pressure	blanket	carbon dioxide			
G gas particles	**H**			**I**	**J**
K	**L** layers	**Alpha-Key Words**		**M** millions of yrs. mesosphere	**N** nitrogen
O oxygen	**P** properties photosynthesis	**Q**	**R**	**S** space stratosphere	**T** troposphere thermosphere
U	**V**	**W** water vapor weight	**X**	**Y**	**Z**

4. Once the key terms have been identified and listed, share with students some different strategies and resources they might use to determine the meanings of unfamiliar words that are listed on the chart. Some of these might include:

　☆ Look immediately before and after the word for a definition that might be included in the text. Often this is set apart by commas or parentheses.

　☆ Using context clues, read the sentence and surrounding sentences to see what makes sense as a definition for the word.

　☆ Check for marginal notes that might explain the word or concept.

　☆ Check the glossary for the meaning of the term.

　☆ Use a dictionary to explore the meaning of the word. .

5. On a transparency, model for students how you use the identified key words and phrases to write a short summary that communicates what the chapter is mainly about. A sample summary might look like this:

Earth's Atmosphere

Our planet is surrounded by a thin blanket of air called the atmosphere, which formed many millions of years ago. It is made up of billions of gas particles, mostly comprised of nitrogen (4/5), oxygen (1/5), and carbon dioxide and water vapor. These gas particles sustain life forms on Earth. The air has certain properties such as space and weight. The atmosphere is divided into four layers: the troposphere where humans live; the stratosphere where planes can fly; the mesosphere, which is the coldest layer; and the thermosphere, which is the hottest.

6. Finally, invite students to complete their own Alpha-Key Words charts, using content material they are reading and following the same process you demonstrated. Extend the lesson by having them practice writing summaries based on their charts.

Writing a glossary

Skills Focus

Analyzing published examples as models for writing

Using organizational features of printed text (glossaries)

Selecting an organized structure/form that best suits purpose

Making appropriate word choices

. . . *as part of the study of science*

Materials & Resources

☆ Short nonfiction books, both with and without a glossary (four or five books per student)

Quick Hints

Invite students to publish a class *Vocabulary Booklet for Nonfiction*, incorporating each of their nonfiction glossaries. They will enjoy reading this booklet during their self-selected reading time, while also reinforcing their knowledge of specialized vocabulary.

STEPS

1. Review with students the role that a glossary plays in informational books. Tell students that in this lesson they will go beyond just making use of a published glossary—they will have an opportunity to develop their own. In doing so, they will learn how to write a concise definition for a word and understand how specialized vocabulary words are related.

2. Divide the class into pairs or small groups and distribute a variety of nonfiction books (as described in Materials & Resources) to each pair or group. Encourage students to examine and explore these books and then to sort them into two stacks—one for books with a glossary and one for those without.

3. Direct students' attention to the books with glossaries. Guide a discussion in which you encourage them to identify the key characteristics of a glossary. On a transparency or the chalkboard, list criteria such as the following:

   ☆ Terms or words are included in alphabetical order in one location at the back of the book.

   ☆ The writing is concise—as much information as possible in a minimal amount of space.

   ☆ A logical pattern is followed.

   ☆ Each definition comprises three parts:
   the term to be defined,
   the class of object or concept to which the term belongs,
   the characteristics that distinguish it from others of its class.

4. Next, on a transparency or the chalkboard, write an example of a simple glossary entry. As volunteers name the key parts of the entry, write in the correct labels. Several samples follow, first as they appear in the content book and then with the parts labeled.

   Water: *a liquid made up of molecules of hydrogen and oxygen in the ratio of 2-to-1.*

   Water (*term*): *a liquid* (*class*) *made up of molecules of hydrogen and oxygen in the ratio of 2-to-1* (*distinguishing characteristics*).

   Caissons: *large steel tubes used in construction and sunk into the earth.*

   Caissons (*term*): *large steel tubes* (*class*) *used in construction and sunk into the earth* (*distinguishing characteristics*).

5. Challenge the pairs or groups to find similar examples in their glossaries and to check for the listed criteria.

6. Finally, have the pairs or groups choose one book from their stack of books that do not contain a glossary. Direct them to read through the book and to select ten important words that connect to the book's main topic. Have them work together to create a glossary of these terms for the book, following the criteria and your examples.

Learning word associations through concept circles

Skills Focus

Writing informational pieces

Planning writing using conceptual maps

Learning new vocabulary

. . . as part of the study of exploration and discovery in the New World

Materials & Resources

☆ Thesaurus (print or online version)

☆ Prepared transparency of the Concept Circle (use model diagram in this lesson to create the transparency)

☆ Photocopies, one for each pair of students, of the Concept Circle

Quick Hints

If students are struggling with the vocabulary, provide them with the three key words by writing these words in the quadrants before they begin categorizing and sorting.

Help with retention by covering each quadrant, one at a time, to test the students' visual memory.

STEPS

1. As preparation for this lesson, select three critical specialized vocabulary words from a unit of content area study. Use a thesaurus to gather several synonyms for each word. The words and synonyms for this model lesson are from a sixth-grade social studies unit on exploration and the New World.

2. Tell students that in this lesson you are going to show them how to make associations among key content terms by using a concept circle organizer. On a transparency of the Concept Circle, list all the words and synonyms in random order under the circle. Read all the words aloud, offering no clue as to the meanings.

3. Divide the class into pairs and distribute photocopies of the Concept Circle, one to each pair. Have students work with a partner to sort the words into three quadrants of the circle. If a word is unknown, they are to write the word in the fourth quadrant labeled "Words I Do Not Know."

4. When students have finished, call on pairs to help you place the categorized words into the pie quadrants on the transparency. Check off words as they are called out. When a pair calls out a word that is unknown, write this word in the fourth quadrant. After all words have been entered into the Concept Circle, discuss with the class which category those unknown words should fall within. During the entire process, guide students as necessary into recognizing the three categories of words. A sample completed Concept Circle is at right:

✔ imperialism	✔ carrack	✔ vessel
✔ mainsail	✔ skirt	✔ authority
✔ masts	✔ detour	✔ caravel
✔ bypass	✔ circumnavigate	✔ influence
✔ power	✔ government	

5. Now take time to discuss the relationships among the words within each category. Circle the key vocabulary word in each quadrant and tell students they will find these words in the unit to be read.

6. Challenge students further by asking them to predict what the reading will be about, based on these vocabulary words.

Exploring the structure of specialized vocabulary words

EXPLANATION: Thinking through the nuances of words helps students develop a familiarity with them; therefore, there's a greater chance they'll use the words in their writing. In this lesson, students use their knowledge of word parts as keys to unlock the meanings of many other words. They also practice writing brief descriptions of relationships among words, tapping into a fairly complex cognitive process.

Skills Focus

Using classroom resources for spelling

Making appropriate word choices

. . . as part of the study of life sciences

Materials & Resources

☆ Dictionary

Quick Hints

At various points during the year, challenge cooperative groups to identify several key words that have meaningful suffixes, prefixes, and bases. Provide the groups with chart paper and colorful markers and invite them to create vocabulary compasses. Have them highlight the common word part and write its definition underneath. Display the charts created in class and encourage students to "visit" the charts to gain word knowledge.

STEPS

1. Review with students the names for word parts—prefix, suffix, and base. Inform them that because so many words in the content areas are specialized terms with roots and affixes, understanding how word parts combine is particularly important in informational reading and writing.

2. Remind students that the strategy of looking at the parts of words and analyzing how the parts combine to make a new word (structural analysis) is useful in their reading as they try to figure out the meanings of unfamiliar words. To refresh their memory of structural analysis, use this example: When readers encounter the word *metamorphic*, they can determine its meaning if they know that the word is made from two meaningful word parts—*meta*, meaning *change*, and *morphic*, meaning *form*. Using deductive reasoning, readers can accurately conclude that metamorphic rocks are those that have changed form. Explain that in this lesson, students will learn to use a vocabulary compass activity that is related to structural analysis. It will enable them to explore words in greater depth so that they can use these terms more easily in their own writing.

3. Using a transparency, write a word from a current content lesson that has one or more meaningful word parts (prefix, suffix, base) and underline the part of the word to be explored. Draw directional arrows that emanate from the word, similar to those on a compass that indicate north, south, east, and west positions.

4. Write the meaning of the word part underneath the compass. Invite students to brainstorm other words with that same word part. Encourage them to use a dictionary. Write these words at the ends of the arrows. Continue to add arrows and words as students call them out. See diagram below:

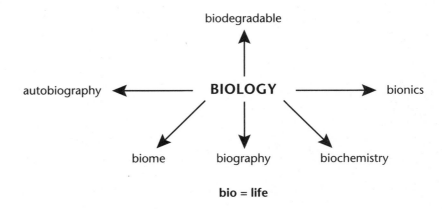

5. Tell students that their next challenge is to decide which word on the compass has the closest relationship to the key word. Begin the process for them by thinking aloud about similarities among a few of the words. For instance, you might say, "*Biography* and *autobiography* are closely related to each other but, except for sharing the same prefix, they are not closely related to the key word. The word *biodegradable* is a little more closely related since it is a science term, which deals with a process of life, the process of decomposing matter. I think, though, that *biochemistry* might be the word with the closest connection to *biology* since both of these are related directly to specific branches of science."

6. When the class has helped you to arrive at the word that you feel has the closest relationship to the key word, directly under the compass write a concise rationale explaining the relationship. Keep in mind that making connections of this sort will involve a great deal of subjectivity. Try not to judge answers as right and wrong as long as students offer logical rationale for their decisions. See the example below.

   Both words deal not only with life, but also with a specific branch of science. One is the study of life science and one refers to the chemistry of living things.

7. When you are sure that students have understood the entire activity, divide the class into pairs and have partners explore several other words in this manner. Encourage students to make use of this technique in future word explorations.

Working with words through poetry: haiku

EXPLANATION: This lesson gives students an opportunity to work creatively with expository terms. Thinking about these words in new and original ways helps students both learn the new vocabulary more deeply, and write in a more interesting, precise manner.

Skills Focus

Writing poems (unrhymed poetry)

Writing in response to what is read and written

Making appropriate word choices

. . . as part of the study of animal habitats

Materials & Resources

☆ Relevant content area terms

☆ Examples of haiku poetry

Quick Hints

Create a display in your classroom library of children's poetry anthologies, especially those that highlight haiku. Encourage children to browse through these anthologies during free time.

STEPS

1. Tell students that in this lesson they will learn about an effective way (that is also a lot of fun) to use new and interesting terms in a subject area. They will have the opportunity to incorporate accurate information into an original haiku poem about that subject.

2. Review with students the content facts and special words they will be using as the basis for their haiku. In this lesson, we use concepts and terms about different animals and their habitats. (See the chart below.)

Habitat	Climate	Shelter	Animals	Food	Water
Wetlands	Very wet Warm	Water Surface marsh Few trees	Fish, frogs, birds, insects, raccoons Opossums Deer	Insects Small animals	Creeks Streams Rivers Lakes Marshes
Arctic zones Tundra	Cold Windy Snowy	Burrows Pits Water	Whales Zooplankton Arctic fox Ermine Bears Arctic tern	Lichen Moss Krill Small animals Adaptive vegetation	Arctic Ocean

3. Model for students the structure of a haiku poem. Remind them that a haiku poem is unrhymed. It is a poem with three lines. Lines 1 and 3 have five syllables. Line 2 has seven syllables. As you write, think aloud about the characteristics of the animal and also the syllables of the words chosen. Below is a model template for a haiku poem and a sample haiku:

_____ (title)

Line 1 _____ _____ _____ _____ _____

Line 2 _____ _____ _____ _____ _____ _____ _____

Line 3 _____ _____ _____ _____ _____

The Arctic Tern

The tern lives in snow.

It migrates through wind and cold.

Krill provides its food.

4. Call on students to help you identify the precise vocabulary you used in your haiku (*migrates* rather than *moves on, krill* rather than *fish)* and discuss with the class how these specific terms impart much more information than the more generic alternatives.

5. Finally, invite students to write their own haiku poems based on content you are studying, employing the process you have modeled.

Working with words through poetry: acrostic poems

Skills Focus

Writing patterned poetry (acrostic)

Using adjectives and adverbs to make writing vivid and/or precise

Using specialized vocabulary

. . . as part of the study of astronomy

Materials & Resources

☆ Relevant content area terms

Quick Hints

You might publish your class book (see Step 6) by placing the final products in plastic sheet protectors and assembling them in a 3-ring binder. Have a volunteer illustrate the cover. House the book proudly in your class and/or share with other classes at your grade level. Just think about how much next year's class will enjoy being introduced to some of the content through this class book! Also, this year's class will enjoy their review of the content through their own creations.

STEPS

1. Another form of poetry that is equally good for combining reading, writing, and content area vocabulary is the acrostic poem. Remind students that in an acrostic poem each letter of the topic is written vertically; it will represent a word or first word of a phrase or sentence that is a descriptive characteristic of the topic. Word choice is particularly important as key aspects of the subject are described.

2. Review the content facts and special words students will be using as the basis for their poems. In this lesson, we use concepts and terms about the properties, locations, and movements of astronomical objects—the sun, moon, stars, planets, asteroids, and comets. This is content that most intermediate students are expected to master.

3. Model for students how you can combine the features of the content words being studied with the creation of an original acrostic poem. As part of the process, demonstrate using a thesaurus to enhance your word choice. You may wish to give students the choice of using individual words or several words to define their subjects. At right is a sample acrostic poem.

   Magnetars

   Magnetic fields of power
   Astronomers measure
   Gamma rays emitted
   New in science
   Energy bursts more powerful than sun
   Thousands of light-years away
   Atoms rearranged by magnetism
   Rapidly rotating in six seconds
   Star shining brighter than others

4. Discuss with students examples of important verbs, adverbs, and adjectives that make the writing interesting. Ask them to analyze the words you've used to see if you've been discriminating in your choices. Would they replace any or are there any important words that don't really relate to the content? (To make the point about precise word usage even more clearly, you might present a "first-draft" version and have students suggest accurate, specific terms that could work better.)

5. Finally, invite students to write their own acrostic poems based on content you are studying, employing the process you have modeled.

6. Consider publishing a class book of poetry on the content that you're studying. Have students choose their own favorite acrostics for this publication. Ask them to peer revise and edit for these items:

   ____ Does my content make sense?
   ____ Did I use precise, descriptive word choices?
   ____ Are there any content inaccuracies?
   ____ Have I defined my subject well?
   ____ Are all words spelled correctly?

Using Graphic/Visual Organizers

There are two familiar adages that can aid our understanding of the power of graphic and visual organizers in the classroom. The first is *Seeing is believing!* In this section, we take a significant step beyond this maxim to suggest through research: *Seeing is also <u>understanding</u>*. In today's classrooms, teachers are increasingly aware that students demonstrate preferences for learning at optimal levels through different modalities—auditory, tactile, kinesthetic, and visual—individual to the learner. With the growing diversity of learners, especially those who are learning English as a second language, we've come to realize how powerful the visual mode of learning is.

The research of Gambrell and Koskinen (2002) reveals that mental images of text benefit learners in two main ways. First, the image provides a framework for organizing and remembering information, which is necessary for comprehension and communication of ideas. Second, the image helps to integrate information across texts, affording learners necessary connections as they process information and enabling them to reorganize and communicate it in different ways.

However, we can't assume that all students will automatically create their own mental images of text or of abstract ideas and concepts. Mental images are a product of students' prior knowledge (Cramer, 1992), and many fourth through sixth graders have quite limited experiences on which to base these critical images. Without some suggestions and coaching by the teacher, many students might not naturally conjure up mental images related to texts. For this reason, it is incumbent upon teachers to instruct students in how to visualize information. One effective method is the use of graphic organizers. Even kindergartners can learn from simple topic maps that a main idea or topic is supported by details, or that a story has somewhat predictable ingredients that interrelate.

Another adage that comes to the forefront in our discussion of graphic and visual organizers is *A picture is worth a thousand words*. Rather than relying upon the thousand words or so that might be necessary to explain the organization of a persuasive piece or the relationships in and among texts, teachers can give students the opportunity to actually *see* the organizational pattern on paper and thus gain a quick understanding of its significance. This organizational picture helps both receptive skills (reading and listening) and expressive skills (writing and speaking). Graphic organizers can be especially helpful in factually heavy informational writing: They provide young writers the opportunity to actually visualize relationships as they map out content in structured paragraphs, sort out opposing positions, compare and contrast ideas, or generate arguments that flow logically.

At this point, we feel it's important to address an obvious question: Is there a chance that students might grow dependent on graphic organizers in their reading and writing? Could graphic organizers used in writing ultimately stifle writers in some way? Unfortunately, we have seen evidence that this can happen. There is a phenomenon that many teachers refer to as "formula writing," in which students write within a certain framework almost as if they were filling in the blanks of a piece of writing. Certainly, these students are not writing as well or as much as they're capable of writing. Sometimes it's apparent that students' originality, voice, and creativity have been sacrificed—for instance, when a first grader inserts the prescribed, transitional word *furthermore* into a composition. Clearly, this isn't the type of writing we want our instruction to result in.

We would suggest that graphic and visual organizers be taught as tools for readers and writers. With this goal, we model here different ways of organizing writing that allow students to practice using the organizer. We wish to underscore that each of these organizers is merely a means to a greater end— something that students can place in their writer's toolbox to use when and if they need it. In fact, this is exactly how proficient writers use these tools. They outline or map or configure as they find it helpful to them. But they are not dependent upon these external organizers because they have formed schema, or mental images, to organize their thinking. We have found that students can be gradually weaned from their dependence on teacher-provided organizers as they build on their new experiences and as they have the opportunity to practice using organizers independently.

An artistic KWL chart helps students organize their thinking and learning related to owl pellets.

Research supports teachers' appropriate use of graphic organizers in reading and writing instruction, and indeed our own experience has proven these techniques useful. In this chapter, we hope you'll find a sampling of graphic tools that you'll enjoy using for powerful results in your classroom.

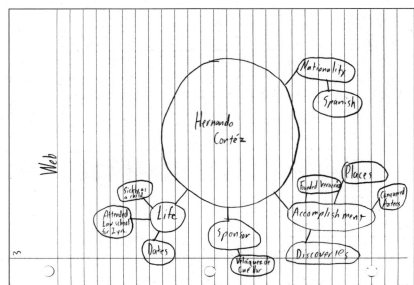

This student has created a simple web to organize information before writing a biographical sketch.

Paragraph planners—paragraphs that compare and contrast information

Skills Focus

Planning writing with details using graphic organizers

Comparing and contrasting facts

Organizing writing into a logical order

. . . as part of the study of contrasting environmental behaviors

Materials & Resources

☆ Fact charts and lists for the relevant content area information

☆ Transparency of the Compare and Contrast Paragraphs graphic organizer

☆ Photocopies, one for each student, of this graphic organizer (see p. 26)

STEPS

1. Tell students that informational writers face a particular challenge: They need to make many different facts fit and flow well together so that their readers can make clear sense of all the information. One way writers can handle the material is by creating comparisons among facts. Graphic organizers can be an effective aid in mapping out paragraphs that contrast information.

2. Review with students the content facts that they will be comparing for a piece of writing. In this lesson, we use facts about migration (see the chart and list below).

Facts:

☆ Instincts help animals meet their needs.

☆ Migration is a behavioral adaptation in which a group of one type of animal moves from one region to another and back again.

☆ Monarch butterflies, the Atlantic green turtles, gray whales, Pacific salmon, and some birds, such as the pectoral sandpiper, are examples of animals that migrate.

Type of Animal	Region	Reason for Migration
Gray whales	Summer at the North Pole Winter in Mexico	For source of food To give birth to young
Pacific salmon	Hatch in rivers/streams Swim to ocean and back to streams	To reproduce

3. Model how to plan a paragraph that contrasts information. First, choose two items to contrast. Then use a transparency of the following graphic organizer to model how you create a paragraph.

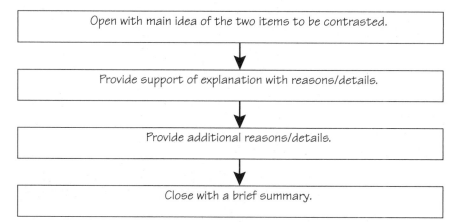

Open with main idea of the two items to be contrasted.

↓

Provide support of explanation with reasons/details.

↓

Provide additional reasons/details.

↓

Close with a brief summary.

For alternative graphic organizers for comparing and contrasting, consider using the formats below. These organizers provide overlapping blocks that encourage students to visualize comparisons. (Each number refers to a source.)

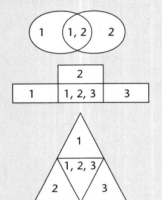

4. Below is a sample paragraph based on the migration facts.

> Gray whales and Pacific salmon are both animals that migrate every year, but they each migrate for different reasons and to different places. Gray whales migrate to find food and to give birth to their young, while Pacific salmon migrate to reproduce. Gray whales travel from the North Pole when summer is over to spend the winter in Mexico. Pacific salmon swim to the ocean and then migrate back from the ocean to the mouth of the river where they hatched, in order to reproduce. Their eggs are laid, fertilized, and hatched in this same area. In summary, while both animals swim and migrate, each has a different reason and a different way of migrating.

5. When you are sure that students have understood the entire activity, divide the class into pairs and have partners complete their own Compare and Contrast Paragraphs graphic organizers (see below), based on appropriate content material. Encourage students to make use of this technique in future content area study.

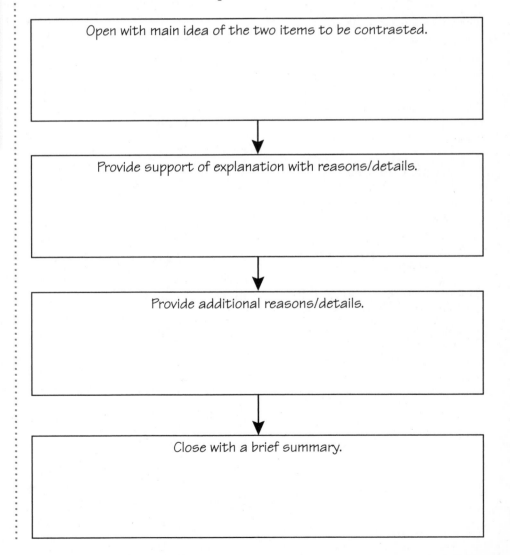

Open with main idea of the two items to be contrasted.

Provide support of explanation with reasons/details.

Provide additional reasons/details.

Close with a brief summary.

Paragraph planners—main ideas and supporting details

Skills Focus

Planning writing with details using graphic organizers

Writing informational pieces

Writing summaries of selections to include main ideas and significant details

. . . as part of the study of thermal energy

Materials & Resources

☆ One sheet of unlined paper for the teacher

☆ One sheet of unlined paper, and pair of scissors, for each student

Quick Hints

This same graphic organizer can be used with narrative text to document clues that demonstrate major literary elements. For instance, one tab can provide information about the main character and another tab can describe the setting.

STEPS

1. Tell students that this lesson will help them to plan their content area writing by using a visual organizer. Many paragraphs in nonfiction writing are structured according to a main idea that is supported by relevant details. This lesson's graphic organizer is especially helpful for constructing those kinds of paragraphs.

2. Take a sheet of unlined paper and fold it in half from top to bottom (widthwise). Write the topic of study on the outside cover of the folded paper in book fashion. The content being studied here is thermal energy, specifically how refrigeration (air conditioning) works. At this point, your model organizer would look like this:

How an Air Conditioner Works

3. Tell students that to organize a paragraph, they must first write a good topic sentence based on the focus of the subject. Open your booklet and, on the left page, write a topic sentence that succinctly includes your main idea:

Topic sentence: An air conditioner works because of the principles of thermal energy.

4. Using a pair of scissors, snip the right page into about five sections, as shown in the diagram below. (Don't cut right up to the fold for best results.) List your supporting details separately on each tab that you've created.

5. Review your supporting details and decide if they all should be included in your paragraph. If not, the tab of the irrelevant detail could be simply torn off and replaced with another paper tab, with a small strip of tape as a hinge.

Topic sentence: An air conditioner works because of the principles of thermal energy.

1) Thermal energy moves naturally from a colder area to a hotter area.

2) Air conditioning uses energy to move heat in a direction it wouldn't normally move.

3) Air conditioning moves heat from inside the house to outside where it is hotter.

4) A refrigerant takes thermal energy from the warm air inside and becomes a gas.

6. Give supplies (paper and scissors) to each student and encourage them to create their own paragraph planners.

Pro/con t-charts

Skills Focus

Organizing writing into a logical order

Planning writing with details using graphic organizers

Writing persuasive pieces for different purposes

. . . as part of the study of economic incentives

Materials & Resources

☆ Transparency of a t-chart

Quick Hints

To make this lesson more dynamic, you might divide the class into two groups. One group is pro the installment plan and one group is con. Call names of students from each side to give supporting facts for their side. Record these on the chalkboard as they are suggested.

STEPS

1. Tell students that in this lesson they will use a t-chart to help them sort out ideas in preparation for writing. Explain that t-charts are particularly helpful for organizing one's thoughts about a controversial or two-sided topic.

2. One such topic is the installment plan, first introduced in the United States after World War I. After reading and studying this plan, discuss with students the pros and cons of the installment plan. List their ideas in a t-chart on the chalkboard or on a transparency. Below is a brief paragraph, intended as a springboard for the more detailed content of a genuine economics lesson. Following the paragraph is a model t-chart that might grow out of the discussion.

> After World War I, the installment plan offered people a way of buying goods when they did not have cash. Advertisements in newspapers, magazines, and on the radio promoted consumer goods.

INSTALLMENT PLAN

Pros	Cons
People could buy goods before cash was available.	People became greedy and could not manage the debt.
Companies and factories sold more goods.	Some numbers were false.
Newspapers and magazines made money advertising these goods.	People were tempted to buy goods they did not need.

3. Once information is sorted out, students may find it easier to decide on their own viewpoint. To extend the lesson, ask students to write a persuasive piece supporting or rejecting the installment plan. A model paragraph (taking the pro side) follows. Note for students how the facts are clearly supported by details and how a strong statement reiterating the main idea concludes the paragraph.

> New shoes, a special basketball, and the latest model car in the garage announce the arrival of the installment plan. Getting something right away that you want is better than having to wait for it. When the newest model car was unveiled, my uncle paid some money down and put the remainder on the installment plan. That way he could drive his new car home that very day. My cousins got new tennis shoes and an autographed basketball in August! Although their family didn't have the cash at that moment, they did not have to wait until Christmas to get these gifts. I think it is a great idea to take advantage of the installment plan.

5 W's graphic organizer

EXPLANATION: This lesson provides a graphic organizer to help students plan out a two-pronged writing assignment. The assignment is to include the 5 W's in a newspaper article written as a first-person eyewitness narrative account with a beginning, middle, and end. Eyewitness accounts are also a wonderful way to make history more immediate.

Skills Focus

Planning writing with details using graphic organizers

Organizing writing into a logical order (choose a point of view based on purpose, audience, length, and format requirements)

Writing effective beginning, middle, and end

. . . as part of the study of human migration and settlement

Materials & Resources

☆ Transparency of a 5 W's graphic organizer (see Appendix, p. 91)

Quick Hints

Suggest additional graphic organizers to collect the 5 W's information. For instance, the outline of a hand with five fingers; a shoebox with the top and four sides available for writing; or a piece of paper folded in half with "five finger strips" cut up to the fold will motivate students to pull together information.

STEPS

1. Tell students that for this lesson they will use a graphic organizer to help them write a special kind of newspaper article—an eyewitness (first-person) account. Explain that all good newspaper articles answer the questions *who, what, why, when,* and *where.* Journalists often refer to these questions as the 5 W's. However, this particular format, the eyewitness account, presents an additional challenge— because it is a narrative story, its details (the answers to the 5 W's questions) should be organized into a beginning, middle, and end. This structure helps the audience visualize the narrator's experiences and the events.

2. Explain to students that they will take the role of an eyewitness during a historical event—for this model lesson the focus is on human migration during the Ice Age. From a first-person viewpoint, students will report how the Ice Age environment affected the lives of the earliest Americans. Below is a brief paragraph, intended as a springboard for the more detailed content of a genuine content lesson on human migration and settlement.

> During the last ice age the nomads followed the animals they hunted for food; they were stopped in Alaska by glaciers. Only when the earth warmed 12,000 years ago did the glaciers begin to melt. At this point, a land bridge called Beringia opened to connect Asia and North America. As the animals moved to new territory, the nomads followed. These nomads were the first people to live in North America.

3. Using a transparency of the 5 W's graphic organizer, think aloud as you consider the facts and map out the newspaper account. A sample completed organizer follows:

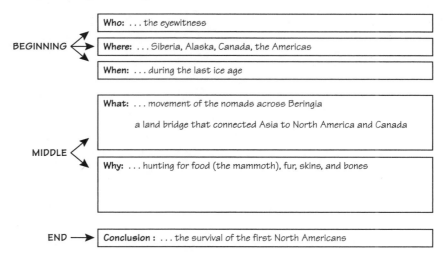

BEGINNING
Who: . . . the eyewitness
Where: . . . Siberia, Alaska, Canada, the Americas
When: . . . during the last ice age

MIDDLE
What: . . . movement of the nomads across Beringia
a land bridge that connected Asia to North America and Canada
Why: . . . hunting for food (the mammoth), fur, skins, and bones

END
Conclusion : . . . the survival of the first North Americans

4. After you model the use of the transparency, engage the class in further discussion. For instance, you might present resource material to help students better understand how these nomads relied on Ice Age animals to survive or how small groups of people had no settled home, but moved slowly (perhaps only a few miles in a lifetime) pursuing food. After the class discussion, encourage students to talk with a partner about daily events that might have occurred during this time period and how the location shaped lives. For instance, they might consider how the nomads built temporary shelters out of wood and skins, hunted for food using spears made from rocks or bones, and made places to sleep from animals' fur. The discussions should help students add depth and detail to their articles.

5. Encourage students to write individual first-person accounts, based on the modeled graphic organizer and the further class discussions. Circulate around the room as students work, checking to make sure that they are following the mapped out logic of the organizer.

Persuasive writing flow chart

EXPLANATION: Writing an effective persuasive piece demands that the writer take a position and support it logically with relevant facts. In this lesson, students use a graphic organizer to help them sort out the facts and create a cogent argument.

Skills Focus

Planning writing with details using graphic organizers

Organizing writing into a logical order (choose a point of view based on purpose, audience, length, and format requirements)

Writing persuasive letters

. . . as part of the study of how geography influences people over time

Materials & Resources

☆ Transparency of the Persuasive Writing flow chart (see Appendix, p. 92)

☆ Photocopies for the class of the flow chart

Quick Hints

An oral debate could precede the writing. Divide the class into two groups. One group argues for the Erie Canal project and the other group argues against it. Set time limits and select a speaker from each group to present their argument. Students may now feel more prepared to plan their letters.

STEPS

1. Tell students that in this lesson they will use a graphic organizer to help them map out their thoughts and feelings about a controversial historical event (for instance, as in this model lesson, the building of the Erie Canal). Once they have established a position and generated substantiating details, they will write a persuasive letter to Mayor DeWitt Clinton of New York City, dated 1817, that is based on the graphic organizer. (You might wish to refer to the lesson on pages 64–66 for fully-developed instructional steps about teaching persuasive letter writing.)

2. Hold a class or small-groups discussion to brainstorm ideas. Use facts and research information such as the essay in the box below as a springboard for the discussion. Encourage students to begin to form an opinion and take a stance as the facts are discussed.

The Erie Canal: Was It Worth It?

In 1817 the New York legislature agreed to fund the Erie Canal to provide a more cost-efficient way to transport goods between the East and the Midwest. Many people doubted that the canal could be built because it would cost millions of dollars to dig and cut through trees and mountains. The New York City mayor, DeWitt Clinton, thought the canal would be good for New York.

Irish immigrants dug most of the canal by hand with shovels, picks, and buckets. These workers had to wear pots of smoking grass around their necks to ward off disease-carrying mosquitoes. They did all this for 80 cents a day, which was a high wage at the time and which attracted thousands of immigrants to the U.S. However, many of these immigrants died during the construction.

Rock had to be blasted and then cut through. Eighteen rivers had to be crossed; therefore, aqueducts and bridges had to be constructed. Eighty-three locks were built to raise and lower the boats and ships.

The canal was completed in 1825. It was 363 miles long and connected Lake Erie to the Hudson River. Once it was open, shipping costs dropped. More people traveled to the Midwest—the trip now lasted days, not months. Hotels and then whole villages, which eventually became big cities, sprang up along the canal. Tolls were charged for use of the canal. Overall, New York State made millions of dollars because of the Erie Canal.

By 1850, railroads began to be built and eventually replaced travel by canal.

---

3. Review writing in a persuasive format. Remind students of these important elements:

☆ Be sure to identify yourself and state your opinion.

☆ Use supporting facts and concrete examples.

☆ Connect ideas using logic and reasoning.

☆ Keep the audience in mind throughout the writing.

4. Present a transparency of the Persuasive Writing flow chart to the class (Appendix, p. 92).

5. Divide the class into pairs or small groups. Distribute a photocopy of the chart to each student. Have them fill in their charts according to the position they decide to take. Remind students that their opinions must be clearly supported by detailed facts. A model completed graphic organizer (taking a stance against the canal) follows:

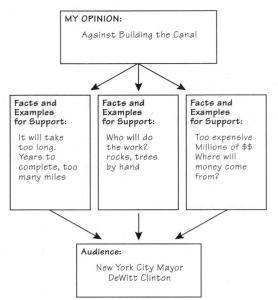

6. To conclude this lesson, have students compose original letters based on their graphic organizers. See the lesson on pages 64–66 for more discussion about writing persuasive letters. A standard business letter format can be used as a template for the letter.

Textual Organizers and Nonfiction Text Patterns

When writing instruction and writing activities are built into all subject areas, students learn better how to reflect on what they are reading and studying. They become dynamically engaged in their content studies, reinforcing comprehension as they are, for example, asked to generate questions about topics or create well-structured outlines based on new information. Often conversation, which can be a springboard for further learning and writing, is also stimulated by these activities. "If children are to become truly literate, they need opportunities to read and write in response to expository texts" (Moss, 1997).

One proven way that we, as teachers, can help our students to improve their nonfiction learning is by giving them direct experiences in observing how authors organize their expository writing around a specific text structure or pattern. This framework helps the student know what to expect and maybe even where to find the information. When a pattern or structure is provided for thinking, a reader's risk of getting lost in the details is greatly minimized. Ellin Keene in *Mosaic of Thought* (1997) calls text "considerate" when it is written in a way that allows its content and format to be predictable or to seem familiar to the reader. She goes on to say that the reader's schema for text format aids in determining the importance of text.

Teachers' guided observation is especially helpful if students are then asked to utilize these same structures and patterns in their own writing. The lessons in this section are set up to help students learn how various text elements, organizers, and patterns work, both in reading and writing. They offer students the opportunity to transfer nonfiction reading skills to writing activities.

Key terms and elements of expository text that readers need to learn to identify in their reading and apply in their writing include: introduction, body, and conclusion; transition and connection words such as *most importantly* or *in conclusion*; the importance of the first and last sentence of each paragraph; concrete examples; italicized or boldfaced words; headings; definitions in the context of a passage. Many of these terms and elements are addressed in this section's lessons.

Reflective readers and writers note differences between narrative and expository text elements and these differences affect the way they comprehend and work with text. In addition, by writing about expository content within a narrative structure (as they are asked to do in one lesson), students can delve into subject matter in unusual ways (for instance, from the point of view of a historical figure or an endangered species) and thereby enhance both content knowledge and writing skills.

Working with expository text patterns is also critical to successful nonfiction reading and writing. One common pattern for dealing with expository text is the question and answer (or Q and A) format. When students write in this format, they activate their prior knowledge of a topic because they are generating questions based on their own curiosity and level of knowledge, and then finding ways to successfully answer the questions. The first lesson in this section focuses on the question and answer format.

Another familiar pattern for nonfiction text is that of cause and effect. In this pattern, the cause is the reason why something happens and the effect is what happens. Time order or sequence of steps is yet another common expository text pattern. In one of this section's lessons, students learn to work with both cause and effect and logical order/sequence patterns while also having the opportunity to decide among different text patterns that will work for the same nonfiction material.

The compare and contrast structure is another important text pattern for nonfiction readers and writers. Some of its common signal words are *different from, similar to, same as, alike, different, although, however, while,* and *unless*. This pattern is treated thoroughly in Section 2, but you might easily modify some of this section's lessons to cover it as well.

Perhaps the most common expository text pattern is that of main idea and supporting details. In this pattern, paragraphs are arranged logically by topics and then expanded with details (both major and minor) that support the topic. The traditional outline format follows the main idea/details pattern. The final lesson in this section gives students the opportunity to work with this pattern, as well as to employ many of the above skills as they craft a well-structured essay based on a thorough outline and incorporating appropriate transitions and connections among ideas.

By learning these and other similar lessons, your students will become better readers *and* writers. And along the way we believe they just might find these activities to be fun!

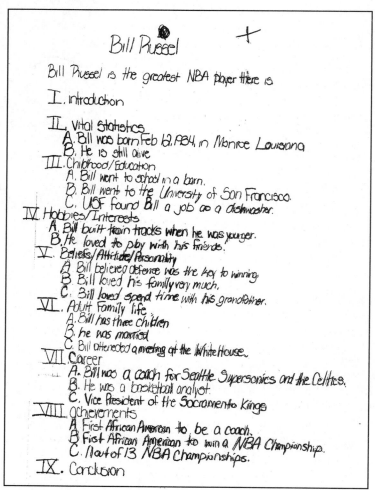

This student decides on the organization, sequence, and priority of main ideas/details for the information he has collected to write a biography.

Organizing by Q and A

EXPLANATION: Students need to learn to recognize that text is organized in a number of different ways, according to purpose. Posing and answering questions is a natural pattern for students to experiment with since their best informational writing is often driven by their curiosity.

Skills Focus

Organizing writing into a logical order (question and answer)

. . . as part of the study of adaptations of living organisms

Materials & Resources

☆ One sheet of paper (unlined or notebook) for each student

☆ Pair of scissors for each student

☆ Content area textbook or informational book

Quick Hints

On the classroom wall, mount a large piece of butcher paper and label it "Things We Wonder" or "Questions We Have." If you use this Q and A method often, allow students to write unanswered questions they have on the paper. These can become great topics for research and writing by all students.

STEPS

1. As preparation for this lesson, have each student fold a sheet of paper in half lengthwise. Next, they each use a pair of scissors to make three to five horizontal cuts from the right edge to the fold. (See diagram below.) Work along with students to make your own tabbed sheet.

2. Tell students that in this lesson they will learn how to pose and answer questions about factual text. In this way, they will be able to use their own curiosity to discover key information. Explain, too, that not only is this Q and A exercise a helpful study technique, but the Q and A writing pattern is also commonly used in expository text.

3. Hold up a content textbook or informational book—for instance, as in this model lesson, a science book about adaptations. Model for students how you examine the title and the cover picture. Think aloud as you record a question you have about that topic on the top line of your paper.

4. Now read a few paragraphs of the text aloud. During your reading, stop occasionally and write any question about the text that has come to mind.

5. Tell students that any time they discover an answer to a question they've written, they should open the tab and record the answer in the space underneath. Model this process yourself with a few of your questions. Below is an excerpt of Q and A writing showing the answer to one of four questions.

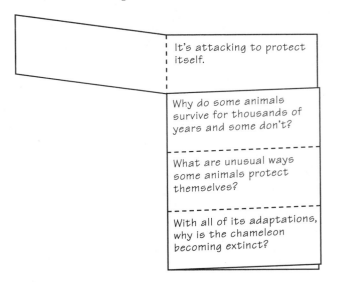

It's attacking to protect itself.

Why do some animals survive for thousands of years and some don't?

What are unusual ways some animals protect themselves?

With all of its adaptations, why is the chameleon becoming extinct?

6. Now, using your Q and A sheet as the basis, model for students how to write a summary of some of the facts you've discovered. A model summary follows:

Animal Sharpshooters

Wow! I learned so many interesting answers to my questions from this chapter of _Animal Sharpshooters_ by Anthony D. Fredericks. First, why do some animals survive for thousands of years while others don't? That was the main point of this text. Many animals are able to make adaptations to their surroundings to protect themselves. For example, the chameleon, which changes its skin color to match its environment, often can't be seen by its predators. Some animals don't make the adaptations and their predators eliminate them.

What are some unusual ways that living things protect themselves? One great example is the sea cucumber that tosses its entire stomach at its enemy when it feels threatened! While its enemy is distracted, it quickly makes a run for it. Smart! Some spiders actually cast their webs to ensnare their enemy, while the bombardier beetle squirts poisonous gas at its attacker.

7. When you have finished demonstrating your own example, invite students to use their own Q and A sheets to engage in this exercise with the class textbook or a selected informational book. Afterward, allow students with unanswered questions to share those with the class to see if anyone knows the answer or if anyone found the answer in his or her text.

8. You might extend this lesson by asking students to write a summary based on their findings.

Using expository terms to organize text

Skills Focus

Organizing writing into a logical order

Writing summaries of reading selections to include main ideas and significant details

. . . as part of the study of earth science

Materials & Resources

☆ Transparency or chart of expository terms

☆ Photocopies of a content area text selection

STEPS

1. Explain to students that in this lesson they will learn how to write a good summary of a piece of expository text by focusing on the structure and logical flow of the text. They will learn how to incorporate terms (primarily but not exclusively verbs) to reflect that same logical order in their summaries.

2. Share with students that many expository compositions follow this structure: introduction of a topic (beginning); discussion and analysis of that topic (middle); conclusion and summary of facts or results (end). When students summarize their expository reading (in book reports, for example) they can use specific terms to help them home in on this structure.

3. Using a transparency or the chalkboard, list some of the most common terms. Group the words as you list them. A sample follows:
   Beginning words: introduce, explore, present, topic
   Middle words: discuss, explain, report, show, analyze, examine
   End words: conclude, surmise, summarize, result

   Encourage students to call out additional words that might be included on this list.

4. Model for students how you summarize a piece of expository writing using these terms and concepts. First, read aloud or distribute photocopies of this text from a book on fossils.

   Fossils are interesting to study. Petroleum (oil and gas) is known as fossil fuel. Most people believe that fossil fuels come from plants that died millions of year ago. The plants became buried and then decayed. Their remains formed fuels. These fuels have been preserved beneath Earth's surface as solids, liquids, and gases.

   Today, people burn fossil fuels for energy. The energy can run cars, make electricity, and heat homes and businesses.

   Fossils are our eyes into the past. As paleontologists find and study more and more fossils, we will know more and more about the Earth's past. Each new fossil fills in a little more of the puzzle of Earth's history. (from _Fossilized_ by Robert Charles, 2002)

5. Now, using a transparency, fill in this Expository Terms Chart to demonstrate for students how you will structure your summary based on the order of the information in the article.

EXPOSITORY TERMS CHART
The **topic** of this book is about fossils.
The author **reports** that fossil fuels come from old plants that were buried and decayed. After long periods of time, these fuels turn into petroleum.
The author **explains** how we use this fuel for energy.
The author **concludes** that fossils help us learn more about the Earth.

Quick Hints

Magazines often contain expository writing that is well constructed, tightly organized, and that delivers a great amount of information in very little space. A few interesting publications include *Ranger Rick*, *Sports Illustrated for Kids*, *Muse*, *Appleseeds*, and *Time for Kids*. Have students find articles that demonstrate how magazine writers use expository terms and logical order to reveal the thrust and organization of their information. Students then make use of this logical order as they construct their own summaries.

6. Create a summary paragraph based on the structure you have set up in the chart. A sample follows:

   In this book the author <u>explores</u> the <u>topic</u> of how fossils are used as fuel for energy. The author <u>reports</u> that these fossil fuels result from old plants being buried and decaying. He <u>explains</u> that we use energy from decaying fossils to run cars and to create heat and electricity. The author <u>concludes</u> that the study of fossils will teach us about the Earth's past.

7. Finally, invite students to follow the procedures you have modeled and to write their own summaries based on content material that the class is studying.

Using narrative story structure with expository material

Skills Focus

Organizing writing into a logical order

Developing plot with well-chosen details

Writing effective beginning, middle, and end (include character, setting, and plot)

Writing narratives that describe and explain

. . . as part of the study of ecosystems

Materials & Resources

☆ Researched facts about a content area topic

☆ Transparencies for story web and model story

☆ Poster of story rubric elements

STEPS

Note: Although we have not broken this lesson into parts, it should be considered a multiday lesson. The focus in the first day is on your presentation and modeling of the elements and story format; on subsequent days, the focus is the students' own content research and story writing.

1. Tell students that in this lesson they will have the opportunity to write a fictional account in story format that is based on content area material they are studying. Although the facts must be accurate, the story is imaginative and thus must be structured according to narrative, not expository, principles. This lesson offers an additional challenge—students' stories will be written in first-person from a particular point of view.

2. Remind students that stories have elements such as character, setting, plot, problem, and solution. They are organized with a beginning, middle, and end. The writer's choice of language and development of voice are also critical. Below is a rubric of characteristics for stories. You might make a poster of this rubric for your classroom.

STORY RUBRIC

1. The story shows the writer's personal voice.

2. The story introduces and develops the characters and setting.

3. The story includes plot, problem, and solution.

4. The story has description and rich details.

5. The story has interesting words and phrases, such as figurative language.

6. Sentences are written in a variety of ways.

---

3. Tell students that an early step in creating their point-of-view stories is gathering and reviewing the important content facts that will form the basis of the story. This particular lesson is based on scientific facts about the impact of the environment on populations of organisms. Thus, for this model story, you have researched facts such as the following ahead of the writing:

Facts About Herons and Swamps

An ecosystem is made up of living things in an environment that can meet their needs. For example, mangrove trees have adapted to survive in an environment in which salty estuary water exists. These trees and their roots provide shelter for gray snapper fish, egrets, and great blue herons.

4. On a transparency or on the chalkboard, model how you map out beginning, middle, and end story structure. Below is an example of how this web might look.

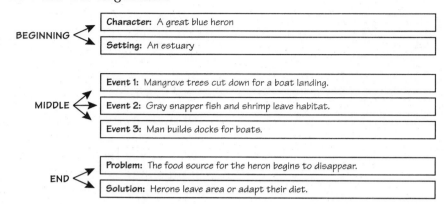

BEGINNING
- **Character:** A great blue heron
- **Setting:** An estuary

MIDDLE
- **Event 1:** Mangrove trees cut down for a boat landing.
- **Event 2:** Gray snapper fish and shrimp leave habitat.
- **Event 3:** Man builds docks for boats.

END
- **Problem:** The food source for the heron begins to disappear.
- **Solution:** Herons leave area or adapt their diet.

5. On a transparency, write a first-person story based on the facts and story web. Point out your incorporation of interesting language, dialogue, and other narrative story features described in the rubric on page 39. Here is a model story:

The Great Blue Heron and the Swamp

"What do you mean there are no shrimp in the estuary!" I yelled to my brother. "We will get very hungry if we stay here," he answered. For several weeks I have been eating with other great blue herons near the mangrove swamp. I love flying near the tree branches late in the afternoon and then swooping along the surface of the water to scoop up the shrimp and gray snappers. There are thousands of tasty morsels just waiting for my brother and me. The water in this estuary is as salty as a pretzel and is teeming with food we love to dine on. Yesterday, we heard loud machines cutting down our mangrove trees. The noise scared off the fish and shrimp, and with the trees disappearing, they have no shelter. Man is building a dock for boats, and it looks like the trees are gone forever. My brother and I will have to fly to another estuary so that we can survive. Now those humans will be catching all the fish!

6. On subsequent days have students research their own material and write their stories. (For lessons and tips on helping students with research work, see Section 4.) To get them started, you might pair them and encourage brainstorming with partners. Conference with them during this brainstorming.

7. Keep posted the story rubric so that students can more easily remember the structure and elements that they need to include. Tell them to remember correct punctuation when using dialogue and to use a variety of sentence structures. Encourage them to illustrate their stories.

Selecting an appropriate text pattern

Skills Focus

Organizing writing into a logical order (select an organized structure/form that best suits the purpose)

Planning writing with details using time lines

Writing in response to what is read and written, using a variety of formats

. . . as part of the study of the impact of how scarcity of resources affects history/ economics

Materials & Resources

☆ Prepared transparency based on researched facts about a content area topic

Quick Hints

To help students make their writing more powerful, encourage them to begin and conclude paragraphs with sentences that are immediate and direct. They should avoid topic and closing sentences that use phrases such as, "This paragraph is about . . .," "I am going to write about . . .," or "My topic is . . . ."

STEPS

1. Explain to students that the same expository text material can be organized in several different ways. As they plan their compositions, writers review the content at hand and select a pattern that organizes the material in a manner that they believe will be the most effective to convey their points. Some of the most common expository text patterns are compare and contrast; logical order and sequence; cause and effect; and main idea with supporting details.

2. Tell students that in this lesson the challenge is to create a well-structured expository paragraph based on certain content. (The content for this model lesson is events in history—from 12,000 years ago until 1915—that have been similarly affected by scarcity of resources.)

3. Use a prepared transparency to present a chart or diagram of the content material (see model chart below). Think aloud about what organizational text pattern would work for a paragraph based upon these facts. (Note: The two that work best for this information are cause and effect, or sequence.)

Time Period	Scarcity	Choice
12,000 years ago	Grasses and animals (which were a food source for humans) were dying out because of climate changes.	To find other food sources, such as fish and wild plants — humans began to learn how to plant seeds.
1682	Lack of abundant sources of land and food in their native European countries	Europeans emigrated to rich land in new colony of Pennsylvania to grow their own food.
1870	Few jobs after the Civil War, slaves not given land to own	Former slaves engaged in sharecropping, or renting land from their former owners.
1915	In South, fewer cotton crops and jobs, lack of education for African-American children	Many African Americans migrated to the North to work in steel and auto factories, and were able to go to school.

4. Model for students how you decide on one format (cause and effect) and begin to organize your thoughts according to this pattern. Start by thinking aloud about a topic sentence that lets the reader know what is coming and states the central cause and effect relationship. For example:

> *As we study history, we find that the economic principle of scarcity and choice has had great effect on people's activities across many thousands of years.*

5. Continue by thinking aloud about the facts highlighted in the chart. These facts will become the basis for the body of your paragraph. Continue to model:

> *As food, land, jobs, and opportunities became scarce, economic decisions had to be made. For example, early peoples moved to find new sources of food when the animals they relied on died off. Many thousands of years later people in certain European countries made a similar decision—to move to a new land where growing food would be easier. These and other choices throughout history were made so that people could find a new region where food and land would be abundant, or where jobs and opportunities flourished.*

6. Now think aloud about the concluding sentence. It should be a strong idea remembered by the reader. For example:

> *As climates change and opportunities decrease, the economic principle of scarcity and choice will continue to affect our world.*

7. Finally, challenge students to select an alternative text pattern for a paragraph based on these facts (chronological sequence). Divide the class into small groups and have students write a new paragraph for the same material that is organized sequentially. Circulate among the groups, helping them as necessary.

Three-Part Lesson: Writing a Well-Structured Expository Composition
Part 1: Creating a main idea/details outline

Skills Focus

Planning writing with details using an outline

Writing in response to what is read and written

. . . as part of the study of the role of entrepreneurs in American history

Materials & Resources

☆ Researched facts about a content area topic

☆ Poster or transparency of expository writing elements

Quick Hints

If you decide to use the model topic in this lesson, other possible entrepreneurs to research are John D. Rockefeller, Cornelius Vanderbilt, Henry Ford, Ray Kroc, Sam Walton, Walt Disney, Anita Roddick, Ted Turner, and Alfred Fuller. An excellent resource for this research is *Business Leaders Who Built Financial Empires* by Jodine Mayberry.

STEPS

1. Tell students that in this multipart lesson, they will first outline and then write a well-structured expository composition. (Depending upon the skill level and readiness of your own class, this composition might be a single paragraph or a multi-paragraph essay.) Writing in the expository mode requires especially careful planning because its primary purpose is to help the reader understand a factual and often complex topic; thus, the writer's goal is to "reason out" an idea(s) for a reader. Well-constructed text that has a clear and logical flow is essential.

2. Review the elements of expository writing with the class. Below is a list of some of the most important of these elements. You might make a poster of this list for your classroom.

ELEMENTS OF EXPOSITORY WRITING

Topic defined—A good topic sentence expresses the main idea.

Unity—Every sentence reveals a single idea that relates to and/or supports the topic sentence.

Coherence (flow)—Sentences build upon one another to create a logical argument or presentation.

Transitions—Every sentence links up naturally with the sentence preceding it. Writers can achieve these transitions by using connecting words or phrases or by repeating key words or synonyms for key words.

Conclusion—A good conclusion wraps up the composition by restating the topic in a manner that ties everything together.

---

3. Explain to students that expository writers typically create an outline to plan and organize their writing. This particular lesson focuses on the role of entrepreneurs in American history. Thus, for this model lesson, present the material in the box below and other related researched material. Discuss the role of entrepreneurs from the Industrial Revolution to present times. Students need to understand that an entrepreneur begins a new business and takes a risk on making a profit or losing money.

Andrew Carnegie, American Entrepreneur

During the early Industrial Revolution steel was needed for railroads and bridges, but it was very expensive. In the 1860s Andrew Carnegie went to Great Britain to observe a process for making steel more cheaply. He brought this new manufacturing idea back to the States and sought out investors. He built a steel mill in

Pittsburgh; it made a healthy profit that he turned over into the purchase of more mills. Carnegie bought coal and iron mines and ships to transport materials, thereby making even more money. He consolidated all of the steel mills into one corporation.

4. On a transparency or on the chalkboard, think aloud as you mull over your factual material to create an outline. Show students how you determine a topic sentence and the major and minor support for the topic. Below is an example of how this outline, based on both the paragraph above and other related research information, might look.

TOPIC SENTENCE: Andrew Carnegie, who made his fortune during the Industrial Revolution, demonstrates many of the main characteristics of a successful entrepreneur.

Major Support	I. Invested in important companies
Minor Support	A. Sleeping railroad car company
Minor Support	B. Oil refinery
Major Support	II. Sought out better ideas
Minor Support	A. Process to make steel stronger and inexpensively
Minor Support	B. Read books on technology
Major Support	III. Strengthened his hold on the steelmaking industry
Minor Support	A. Bought coalfields, iron ore mines, and steamships
Minor Support	B. Consolidated other steel mills with his own

5. Point out to students that statements I, II, and III offer direct explanations of the topic sentence. They can double-check this by inserting the word *because* between the topic sentence and the major support statements. Likewise, the minor support statements A and B act as examples that explain and prove the major support. Inserting the word *because* illustrates a sound and logical connection with the major statement.

6. After your modeling and a discussion of the outlining process, invite students to begin to gather information on the topic (in this case, entrepreneurs). Provide class, library, and computer time for students to conduct research in textbooks, trade books, and online. Encourage students to select one entrepreneur who particularly intrigues them. Remind them that the ultimate goal of this lesson is to write a well-structured expository piece based upon their research.

Three-Part Lesson: Writing a Well-Structured Expository Composition
Part 2: **Using transitions to connect ideas**

EXPLANATION: The outline modeled in Part 1 of this lesson provides an ideal springboard for students to work with transitions and connections. Here, they learn to take the relationships they have outlined and use certain words and language conventions to express them in writing.

Skills Focus

Using conjunctions to connect ideas

Using transitions to connect ideas

Writing in response to what is read and written

... as part of the study of the role of entrepreneurs in American history.

Materials & Resources

☆ Transparency of outline from Part 1 of this lesson

☆ Transparency of transitions and connections

Quick Hints

Using your social studies textbook or other informational sources, select text that illustrates the methods described in this lesson. Read aloud statements and ask students to identify which of the two methods the author(s) used to achieve transition.

STEPS

1. As students continue their research and work on their outlines, conduct this mini-lesson on the importance of transitions and connections in expository writing. Point out that the logical order of the major and minor statements in the outline is the cohesive thread that makes the entire composition hold together. Thus, the expository writer must make the relationships among supporting statements as clear and as strong as possible.

2. Review with students that writers achieve these transitions and connections in several different ways. On a transparency or the chalkboard, present the two possible means described below:

   METHOD #1: Using words or phrases to show relationships

   Example: Andrew Carnegie was an entrepreneur. <u>Therefore</u>, he probably took business risks.

CHART OF COMMON TRANSITION WORDS	
Addition	and, also, in addition, furthermore, moreover
Contrast	but, yet, however, still, although, though, nevertheless, on the other hand
Time	first, second, next, then, finally, later, when, after, before, until, a few days later, at the same time
Position	behind, here, there, around, next to, to the right of, down, up, close to
Cause and Result	therefore, thus, as a result, consequently
Manner or Method	thus, for example, similarly, in this way
Condition	if, unless, until

   METHOD #2: Repeating key words or their synonyms. These key words are usually the subject and the controlling idea.

   Example: Andrew Carnegie was an entrepreneur. This wealthy man had a knack for making businesses turn a profit.

3. By the conclusion of Part 2 of this multipart lesson, students should have completed their research and developed a topic sentence as well as a simple outline of information they wish to convey to the reader. Encourage them to begin to map out the connections and transitions they will utilize as they write their compositions.

Three-Part Lesson: Writing a Well-Structured Expository Composition
Part 3: **Writing the composition**

EXPLANATION: Now that students have compiled their information, completed their outlines, and worked with transitions, they are ready to write. This lesson gives them the opportunity to put it all together in their own well-structured expository compositions.

Skills Focus

Using conjunctions to connect ideas

Using transitions to connect ideas

Writing in response to what is read and written

. . . as part of the study of the role of entrepreneurs in American history

Materials & Resources

☆ Photocopies, one for each student, of your outline from Part 1 of this lesson

☆ Students' individual research and outlines from Parts 1 and 2 of this lesson

Quick Hints

As students continue to write additional expository pieces, heighten their awareness of transitional words and phrases. Ask them to use a highlighter to mark transitions used in their first drafts.

STEPS

1. Quickly review the previous days' lessons. Call on volunteers to explain the importance of the topic sentence, the hierarchical relationships demonstrated by an outline, and the way in which expository writers show transitions and connections in their compositions.

2. Distribute photocopies of your outline from Part 1. Have students refer to the outline as you use a transparency to model writing an expository piece based upon it. Think aloud about the transitions you are using throughout your model writing. Below is an example of a paragraph based on the outline.

Andrew Carnegie, American Entrepreneur

<u>Andrew Carnegie</u>, who made his fortune during the Industrial Revolution, demonstrates many of the main characteristics of a successful <u>entrepreneur</u>. <u>Carnegie</u> began to <u>make money</u> by investing in important companies. <u>First</u>, he realized the need for railroad transportation so he <u>put his money</u> in a railroad sleeping car company. <u>Later</u>, he <u>invested</u> in an oil refinery. <u>As a result</u> of the profits made from investments, Carnegie traveled to Great Britain and observed a process used to make steel stronger and a way to produce steel in an <u>inexpensive way</u>. He brought these <u>new ideas</u> to his mills in the United States. <u>In addition</u>, he read every book on technology to assist in the development of his business. By buying coalfields, iron ore mines, and steamships, he strengthened his hold on the steel industry. <u>As a result</u> of these <u>acquisitions</u>, Carnegie was empowered to buy other steel mills, consequently consolidating them to form a large new corporation. As an <u>entrepreneur</u>, <u>Carnegie</u> realized <u>great wealth</u> while he developed one of the most productive companies in United States history.

3. With students' help, go back through the piece to identify the transition words as well as the key words and phrases that are repeated or for which synonyms are used. Underscore these words and phrases, as shown in the example, to help reinforce the connections.

4. Finally, invite students to use their outlines to write their own expository pieces. Circulate in the class as students work, checking to make sure they are adhering to their outlines and using appropriate transitions to achieve coherence.

Putting Research Skills to Work

As students read and write in the content areas, their curiosity about the world around them grows. As educators, we become excited as these students begin to ask more questions about the texts they are studying. These questions naturally lead to research. When utilized most effectively, this research further connects students to a specific topic of interest. Research writing serves many purposes, such as explanation, entertainment, helping students process information, and connecting writers more deeply with what they're reading. Some of us can recall the days when a research assignment resulted in copying, or at best paraphrasing, words from the World Book Encyclopedia. There was minimal note-taking, summarizing, questioning, or organization of the information. Thankfully, things have come a long way since then! In this section, we will take a look at specific mini-lessons that will enable the student to participate appropriately in a research activity.

From the very beginning of a research project, well-focused instruction can help—for many students spend an inordinate amount of time selecting a topic. And even after they've chosen a topic, it may be so broad that they find it impossible to organize the resulting information. Thus, teachers can help students to learn how to select and then to narrow their research topic so that it is more specific and tightly drawn.

Once they've established a topic, students need to develop questions that will drive their research. These questions should be open-ended—not answered with a simple *yes* or *no*. The depth of the questions will determine whether critical thinking and genuine learning can take place. If students generate probing questions about a scientific investigation, they will be more likely to gather meaningful data as they seek the answers—data that can then be organized in a manner that permits a pattern of similarities and differences to emerge. Like science, social studies should involve exploration of open questions that require higher-level thought processes. The key social studies subjects—history, economics, government, geography, and culture—are all available as topics for inquiry. Questions addressing these topics invite discussion, which is often best accomplished through cooperative group work. The answers to these questions are rarely in the textbook but require students to investigate other sources to arrive at possible answers or opinions.

Students need to become adept at reading vast quantities of information and summarizing it. Summarizing, which is the skill of creating brief statements from lengthy pieces, makes information manageable by helping learners focus on the key points to be retained. As part of summarizing, students use headings, key words, main ideas and important details from text, as well as posing questions like, "What is the author talking about in this part?"; "What is this paragraph all about?"; or "What is important to remember?"

A guide, provided by the teacher, helps students to take notes and prioritize information that they are researching and gathering.

Students also need to learn how to take notes from various sources so that they can commit what they've read to their knowledge base. They are writing for themselves as they record information. These notes also can be taken when listening to selections they have heard read aloud, when watching videos, or when listening to guest speakers. As always, if the teacher models the note-taking process, it will not seem so difficult.

Another important research writing skill is knowing how to transcribe and record scientific observations. As part of such observations, individuals or groups list what they know and what they recall from personal experience with the investigation; generate questions; keep track of data and variables; compare hypotheses; etc.

The lessons in this section address all of the skills described above. When our students are shown models of good research writing, when they are taught through mini-lessons that address their specific needs, and when they are allowed to choose topics of their own interests, remarkable expository writing will follow.

Information about famous African Americans is published on dynamic charts created by students.

Developing open-ended questions

EXPLANATION: Questions guide research. Many students have difficulty with designing questions that will lead to in-depth study. Harvey and Goudvis (2000) differentiate between "thick" and "thin" questions. Our goal as teachers is to have students design thick questions that require a search through multiple materials and therefore provoke interesting responses. Thin questions, the sort that can be answered with a simple yes or no, will not lead students to engage in good research.

Skills Focus

Writing informational pieces

Framing questions to direct research

Responding in constructive ways to others' writings

. . . as part of the study of earth science

Materials & Resources

☆ Science or social studies textbook

Quick Hints

Ask students to label end-of-unit textbook questions as "thick" or "thin." Mark the answers to the thin questions by using narrow strips torn from a sticky note. For thick questions, attach a whole sticky note and have students write the answer on this note.

STEPS

1. Explain to students that the way they set up their questions for research work will have a major effect on the research itself. The way they word a question can lead them to one kind of response or another. Tell them that some questions are thin. Thin questions require only a surface-level or literal-level response; they usually begin with *who, what, where, when, how many*, etc. Thick questions, on the other hand, require a deeper, more thoughtful response and usually begin with *why, how, might, what caused, for what reasons*, etc. (See this lesson's Explanation for more about thick and thin questions.)

2. Inform students that in this lesson they will have an opportunity to practice generating their own questions orally in response to their reading. Their goal will be to generate thick, not thin, questions.

3. Model by reading a paragraph aloud from a science or social studies text and thinking aloud of a thick question and a thin question that the information answers. A sample paragraph and an example of a thick question and a thin question follow.

   The movement of the mantle of the earth makes the plates move. They move apart, slide against each other, and collide. This sliding and colliding causes huge layers of rock to be pushed up. It causes mountains to be formed. (from *Fossilized*, by Robert Charles, 2002)

   Thick question: "How does this movement relate to earthquakes?" (Requires inference and possibly an extended search for more information.)

   Thin question: "What causes the plates to move?" (This answer is right there in the text and is easily found.)

4. Repeat this process with the class a few more times, using different content paragraphs and eliciting responses from volunteers. Ask for examples of each kind of question, label them "thick" or "thin," and discuss and examine them with the class. Students will begin to feel more comfortable the more this is performed orally.

5. Now divide the class into small groups or pairs. Have students select a new topic and read at least two paragraphs from the text. Their goal as a group or a pair is to write two thick questions. As a follow-up extension to this lesson, assign students to answer their own questions through further reading and research.

Two-Part Lesson: Organizing Information for Writing
Part 1: Using a research organizer for taking notes

EXPLANATION: As students become familiar with gathering and writing informational text, using the simple organizer in this lesson makes the process painless and manageable. The organizer that they create in this part of the lesson leads them seamlessly to the composition they write in the lesson's second part.

Skills Focus

Planning writing with details

Organizing writing into a logical order

Taking notes from authoritative sources

Locating information

. . . as part of the study of weather

Materials & Resources

☆ Transparency of Research Organizer (Appendix, p. 93)

☆ Two-sided photocopies, one for each student, of the Research Organizer (p. 93)

☆ Content resources, such as a textbook

Quick Hints

Invite students to create their individual research organizers. Have them cut apart their two-sided copies on the dotted lines and then staple the pages together. Note that students' free-writes will occur on the back side of the notes pages.

STEPS

Note: Throughout this lesson, refer to page 51 for a sample completed research organizer.

1. Tell students that in this lesson they will learn to use a simple and efficient method for gathering information, taking notes on important ideas and concepts, and organizing the information for greater understanding.

2. Using a transparency of the Research Organizer form and a preselected textbook chapter, demonstrate for the class how you record the major topic in the space provided at the top of the form. For example, write "Making Weather Predictions."

3. Next, skim for and read aloud the chapter's headings. Model how you turn these headings into questions. List them underneath the topic on the first page of the organizer form. For example, "Measuring Weather" becomes "How is weather measured?"

4. After you have rephrased all the headings as questions, read the questions aloud and decide on the three you're most interested in. Think aloud to demonstrate your decision-making process for the class. Strike a line through the questions that you won't pursue.

5. Next, transcribe each of the three questions that you will be using to the top line of a separate section of the organizer (one question per section). Thus, the question, "How is weather measured?" becomes the heading for the section marked page 3, and so on.

6. Read aloud the textbook material that corresponds to the first question. Using the section marked page 3, make note of key ideas and concepts and write appropriate words or phrases next to the bullets on the form.

7. Direct students' attention to the section labeled "Here's what I've learned about Question 1:" (p. 4) and model for students how you use your notes for that question to free-write an answer on the lines provided. (Be sure to use full sentences in your writing to show the transformation from informal notes to real drafting.) Use this same process for the next two questions until you've completed all parts of your transparency booklet. A completed organizer is on page 51.

8. Distribute a two-sided photocopy of the Research Organizer form (Appendix, p. 93) to each student. Work with students to help them create their own organizer booklets. (See directions in Quick Hints and on page 93.)

Research Organizer

Front Side of Form

TOPIC: Making Weather Predictions

Questions I have about this topic:

How is weather measured?
How do scientists map and chart weather?
~~What factors affect humidity?~~
~~What is dew point?~~
~~What instruments are used to measure weather?~~
What symbols are used on weather maps and what do they mean?
~~What properties of the atmosphere affect our weather?~~

1

QUESTION 2: How do scientists map and chart weather?

Notes: Watch and measure conditions
Analyze the data
Mark symbols on their maps
Keep track of moving air masses

5

QUESTION 1: How is weather measured?

Notes: Meteorologists measure and study
Conditions: air temperature, air pressure, wind speed and direction, humidity
Tools: barometer (air pressure), anemometer (wind speed), thermometer (temperature)
Satellite pictures study clouds/conditions

3

QUESTION 3: What are the symbols used on weather maps and what do they mean?

Notes: long lines with triangles or half circles = fronts
words or symbols = weather in an area
small dashes = rain
small stars = snow
various marks = types of clouds

7

Back Side of Form

What I've learned about Question 2:

Scientists constantly watch and measure weather conditions, keeping track of air masses. As the scientists track, they record their findings on maps and charts so that they can analyze the data. They use a system of symbols to record the data.

All of this helps them to predict weather patterns.

6

(This page is blank.)

2

What I've learned about Question 3:

The symbols used by scientists who study the atmospheric changes are rather simple. They use long lines with semicircles and triangles for different types of fronts. Sometimes words are used to represent the weather in regions, such as hot or cold. Small dashes stand for rain, and stars represent snow. Various marks are used to represent different types of clouds.

8

What I've learned about Question 1:

Meteorologists are responsible for measuring and studying weather. There are several weather conditions that guide them. Those are air temperature, air pressure, wind speed and direction, and humidity. Certain tools help them to calculate their measurements. For example, they use a barometer to measure the air pressure and an anemometer to figure the wind speed. Satellites record pictures of clouds and systems that they can analyze.

4

Two-Part Lesson: Organizing Information for Writing

Part 2: **Writing a summary from organized notes**

EXPLANATION: In Part 2 of this lesson, students learn to translate the Research Organizer into an organized summary piece to convey what they've learned. They'll be surprised at how easy the transformation occurs!

Skills Focus

Planning writing with details

Organizing writing into a logical order

Writing informational pieces

. . . as part of the study of weather

Materials & Resources

☆ Research Organizer from Part 1 of this lesson

☆ Students' Research Organizer booklets from Part 1 of this lesson

☆ Lined transparency for writing

Quick Hints

The Research Organizer in this lesson can be used with any content material. It can help guide students through reading any of their textbooks, taking notes, and then summarizing the notes to clarify meaning and deepen understanding.

STEPS

1. Review briefly with students the free-write paragraphs on your transparency from Part 1 of this lesson. Tell students that today you'll show them how you transform your information into a summary piece that conveys what you've learned.

2. Model how page 1 of the organizer becomes the basis for your introduction. Then use the free-writes on pages 4, 6, and 8 for the body of your paper, and return to page 1 to recap for your conclusion. Below is a summary based on the organizer on page 51.

Weather Forecasting

Will it rain tomorrow for our picnic? Let's turn on the television and find out from a person who spends a great deal of time studying atmospheric conditions. How do they do it? Here are a few things we know about how weather is studied, how it's mapped and charted, and even some of the common symbols used.

Meteorologists are responsible for measuring and studying weather. There are several weather conditions that guide them. Those are air temperature, air pressure, wind speed and direction, and humidity. Certain tools help them to calculate their measurements. For example, they use a barometer to measure the air pressure and an anemometer to figure the wind speed. Satellites record pictures of clouds and systems that they can analyze.

Scientists constantly watch and measure weather conditions, keeping track of air masses. As the scientists track, they record their findings on maps and charts so that they can analyze the data. They use a system of symbols to record the data. All of this helps them to predict weather patterns.

The symbols used by scientists who study the atmospheric changes are rather simple. They use long lines with semicircles and triangles for different types of fronts. Sometimes words are used to represent the weather in regions, such as hot or cold. Small dashes stand for rain, and stars represent snow. Various marks are used to represent different types of clouds.

So, it's easy for us to turn on the television to find out the forecast. However, we should realize that someone has spent a great deal of time studying weather systems, mapping and charting the conditions, analyzing data and symbols—all in an effort to let us know if we can have our picnic tomorrow!

4. Invite students to use their own organizers to take notes from a content source, generate free-write paragraphs based on the notes, and compose an organized summary from these notes, following the modeling and samples you have provided. This part of the lesson might extend several additional days.

Narrowing a research topic using a table of contents

Skills Focus

Generating ideas

Using organizational features of printed text (table of contents, indexes, etc.)

. . . as part of the study of China in social studies

Materials & Resources

☆ Several related science or social studies books with tables of contents

Quick Hints

When your students are ready for a more detailed means of narrowing a topic, introduce them to the index and guide them through its use, helping them to see how it lists topics in an even more specific way than the table of contents. Remind students to use this additional resource in their future research work.

STEPS

1. Tell students that one of the most challenging and important aspects of research happens at the very beginning of the process. The topic selected for research can affect the nature and quality of the research itself. Inform students that a subject that is too broad and undefined simply doesn't lend itself as well to careful examination. Call on volunteers to help you figure out which would be a more focused topic for research: "Dogs" versus "How did wolves evolve into dogs?" Or how about "Sports" versus "What is the history of baseball in the U.S.?" Discuss with the class why, in each case, the second topic is more conducive to fact finding and fruitful exploration. Tell students that this lesson introduces a procedure to assist them in narrowing a research topic so that it is more specific and tightly drawn.

2. Begin the process by having students help you generate a list of topics. Tell students that they should suggest topics that they wish to know more about and that they find interesting. Below is a sample list of topics that an intermediate-grade class might generate for science and another for social studies.

Science Topics	Social Studies Topics
animals	immigrants
earthquakes	pioneers
planets	China
rocks	the West
weather	the American Revolution

3. Next, model for students how you select a topic from among these possibilities. Think aloud as you weigh the topics in terms of interest and knowledge. For this lesson, we focus on the topic of China. After selecting China as the area of research, model further how you can move from such a broad area to one that is very specific. To demonstrate this narrowing, choose a book about China from the preselected set of information books (see Materials & Resources). Holding the book up, show the class how you locate and read the table of contents. A sample book and its table of contents follow:

 Book: *Postcards from China by Zoe Dawson*
 <u>Table of Contents:</u>
 ☆ Bikes in Beijing
 ☆ Chinese Food
 ☆ The Forbidden City
 ☆ The Great Wall
 ☆ The Longest River

☆ The Biggest City

☆ Chinese New Year

☆ The Chinese Flag

4. Now model for students how you select one topic from among these chapters. As before, think aloud as you weigh the topics in terms of interest and knowledge. Ultimately, decide on one of these specific subtopics about China, for example, the Great Wall.

5. Finally, challenge the class to explain why this topic is much narrower than the broad topic of China. With students' help, generate a set of well-focused questions that can be used to guide subsequent research. For example:

☆ Why was the Great Wall built?

☆ How long did it take to build?

☆ What does it represent to the people of China?

6. When students need to decide on their next content area research project, encourage them to put this procedure to use in their own work.

Summarizing

Skills Focus

Organizing writing into a logical order by selecting an organized structure that best suits purpose

Writing summaries of reading selections to include main ideas and significant details

Responding in constructive ways to others' writing

. . . as part of the study of ecosystems

Materials & Resources

☆ Relevant content facts and data appropriate for summarizing

Quick Hints

Tell students that using important vocabulary words will aid them in summarizing. Have them practice by finding paragraphs from science or social studies texts and then selecting key words or phrases to sum up the paragraph in one or two sentences.

STEPS

1. Review with students the basic elements of a summary: It is a concise composition that sums up the gist of a body of information and that must include the main idea and the most important (not simply interesting) facts. Tell students that in this lesson they will have the opportunity to summarize data from a chart. This process will allow them to put the information into their own words. By doing so, they will also find that the facts themselves are easier to remember.

2. Review with students the content facts they will be using as the basis for their summary. In this lesson, we use concepts about animal adaptations (see the chart below).

Animal	Feature: Body Coverings	Niche in Ecosystem
Birds	Lightweight feathers	Protect from wetness, cold weather, and aid in flight
Fish	Scales	Protect from disease and prey
Reptiles (iguana)	Scales	Protect from injury and drying out
Snake	Scales	Overlap to aid in movement
Polar bear	Hair	Clear color—allows light to get to dark skin to keep animal warm On feet to aid in walking on ice and snow
Bison	Fur	Sheds winter fur in summer
Dolphins	Small amount of hair	Aids in gliding through water
Hedgehog	Hair	Spinelike and sharp for protection

Animal	Feature: Color/Shape	Niche in Ecosystem
Lemmings	Nose	To tunnel under snow to keep warm
Snowshoe hare	Fur	White in winter, brown in summer
Tiger	Fur	Striped to blend in with light and shadows of tall grasses
Toads	Skin	Bumpy, brownish like pebbles on forest floor
Chameleon	Skin	Changes color to match surroundings

3. There are a number of ways that the data from a chart like this might be summarized. Demonstrate for students your thinking process as you select one section to summarize—for instance, "Body Coverings." Continue to model how you decide on the main idea. Explain that summaries often begin with an important statement, followed by important details.

4. Using a transparency, model writing a summary of the facts that describe this aspect of how animals adapt to their environment. In addition to the proper format of a summary, focus on using vivid adjectives. A sample summary is below:

> **How Body Coverings Help Animals Adapt to Their Ecosystems**
>
> Animals adapt to their ecosystems. Different body coverings are the key to their survival. From the thick hair of a polar bear or bison, to the soft feathers of an eagle, to the bumpy scales of an iguana, fish, or snake, these coverings protect from cold and dry climates, as well as aid in movement. The scales of reptiles and the spinelike sharp hair of a hedgehog offer protection from injury. Body coverings support animals in various habitats and allow them to survive as species.

5. Finally, invite students to discuss a different aspect of the content facts with a partner for a few minutes. Explain that after this discussion they will select a topic to summarize. For example, in this lesson, they could choose to summarize "Color/Shape" from the fact chart.

Making scientific observations

EXPLANATION: In the study of science, developing a keen eye for observations is critical. Having students keep a journal of their observations of experiments and of their responses to new information helps them process new knowledge. In this lesson, you'll model for students different ways that they can notate their observations in journals.

Skills Focus

Writing informational pieces

Evaluating research

Raising new questions for further investigation

Writing in learning logs and journals to discover, develop, and refine ideas

. . . *as part of the study of energy and matter*

Materials & Resources

☆ Transparency of Scientific Observations form (p. 58)

☆ Objects for simple scientific experiment: for this example, beaker and water

Quick Hints

In lieu of using forms for students to document their observations, you can cut marble composition books (with sewn binding) in half widthwise. Each book becomes two convenient, attractive response or documentation journals. Your local hardware store or any print shop can cut these for you.

STEPS

1. Review with students the critical importance in any scientific work of a scientist's making careful, precise observations. Discuss with the class why this skill is so essential. Discuss, too, that like any skill, it needs to be learned and practiced. Explain further that writing down their observations will help students greatly in this learning—it is an effective way of focusing attention on scientific details, as well as reinforcing new scientific knowledge. Tell students that in this lesson they will observe a simple scientific experiment and record their observations and findings on a special form.

2. Before beginning the experiment, review key content terms with students. In this lesson, the focus is on energy transfer and the key terms are

   ☆ **Energy**—the ability to cause change
   ☆ **Evaporation**—the changing of liquid into gas
   ☆ **States of matter**—solid, liquid, gas

3. To conduct the experiment, place 250 milliliters (8 oz.) of water in a beaker in a sunny place in the classroom. Explain to the class that the scientific purpose of this experiment is to observe the transfer of energy and why evaporation occurs. This experiment will be recorded over a period of time.

4. Using a transparency based on the Scientific Observations form on page 58, model the process you engage in to make and record observations.

5. Walk students through each step of the form. For "Part I: Snapshot," tell students that this is the place for a clear pictorial representation of what the experiment looks like at the very beginning. They should create a simple drawing to depict what they see.

6. As you complete "Part II: I Observed...," comment to students that this part needs to be totally factual—no opinions or conclusions. You only report exactly what the eye sees. They should also include even those elements that seem to have no relationship to the experiment, such as particles that may have blown into the beaker. Explain that something that appears to have no bearing may ultimately be a factor.

7. As you model completing the next step on the form, "Part III: I Wonder...,' share with students that, based on observations you've made, you'll now formulate questions that have piqued your curiosity about what you've observed. Tell them you won't worry at this point about whether or not each of your questions will be answered in this experiment. Write your questions on the form.

8. Point to "Part IV: I Predict." Tell students that you need to call on all that you know about water, evaporation, and weather to make predictions about what changes might occur over a period of time with the water in the beaker. Record your predictions on the form.

9. Finally, model filling in the last step on the form. Remind students that this experiment will be conducted over a period of days/weeks and that today's documentation probably will not reveal any dramatic conclusion. However, no matter how insignificant the results might seem, you need to record them just as scientists record everything they observe (even the fact that no changes have occurred) about their experiments.

10. Here is a sample completed form:

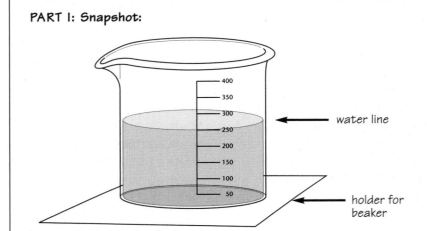

PART I: Snapshot:

water line

holder for beaker

PART II: I Observed...

The water line is exactly at the 250-milliliter mark on the side of the beaker. The water is crystal clear with no bubbles. The beaker is in a sunny window.

PART III: I Wonder...

As the sun warms the beaker, what will happen to the water level?

Will the water change at all? How quickly will the water evaporate?

Will outside and inside temperatures affect evaporation?

PART IV: I Predict...

I think that the water level will decrease and that bubbles will form in the water.

PART V: What Happened:

Because little time has gone by, there are no observable changes in the experiment today.

Writing for Authentic Purposes

Students are far more likely to invest time in their writing if the topic and purpose for writing matter to them and if they are writing for a real audience. Publication of student writing is vital: When given the opportunity to "publish" their work, students grow markedly as writers (Zemelman, Daniels, and Hyde, 1998). Publishing extends their audience beyond school walls. How excited our students are when their writing is displayed at the shopping mall, in the local public library, or in a doctor's waiting room!

Students are drawn more attentively into content material, as well as into the writing process itself, when they use writing as a tool to further content area understanding. After reading content material, students need an opportunity to apply writing strategies to help them make sense out of what they have read and to commit new learning to their personal knowledge base. The mini-lessons in this section focus on writing for authentic purposes that tie into science and social studies content.

By putting themselves in the place of a character from history—John Smith, for example—and writing an original speech from that character's point of view, students are better able to reinforce the information learned, in this case the Jamestown colony.

Students at this age have very strong opinions and are eager to argue with one another or their parents and teachers about a specific point of view. This curiosity and tenacity can be tapped into when teachers ask them to outline facts and opinions and compose well-structured persuasive letters and editorials. Writing a letter to persuade someone to take a particular action—for example, to enter into a trade agreement with benefits on both sides—enables students to personalize newly acquired content knowledge. Or, if students feel strongly about an environmental issue, they can be encouraged to write persuasive letters to a government agency or to the editor of a newspaper. In social studies, as taxes are examined through a unit on economics, students may feel compelled to write to their congressional representative to offer a viewpoint.

By providing students with expository writing assignments that connect to their lives, we are encouraging them to develop their own voice, even in the often arid arena of informational writing. William Zinsser addresses voice in his book *On Writing Well: the Classic Guide to Writing Nonfiction*:

"Writers are obviously at their most natural when they write in first person."

The lessons in this section are aimed at helping students learn that expository writing is an art, an art that incorporates a personal but polite and formal voice.

In addition to the writing assignments mentioned above, there are numerous other kinds of compositions that lend themselves to providing students with authentic purposes for writing. Following is a sampling of other possibilities. Several of these are addressed in this section; others are included here to encourage you in your own brainstorming. The list is almost endless!

Admit or Exit Slips: These ticketlike items ask students to summarize what they have learned the day before as they enter the classroom or begin a new lesson, or to pose questions about the present day's lesson as they leave the classroom or begin another subject study.

Dialogue Journals/Letters: As a way of reflecting and clarifying information, students use a journal, learning log, or letter format to write to a peer or to the teacher as a response to text read.

Group Investigations: Students work with others to share, discuss, and write about their findings. This technique is often used following a scientific observation activity.

Directions: Writing directions helps students understand the importance of logical order and sequence. They might be asked to write directions for a process activity in science or to provide directions to make a map for a geography lesson.

Alphabet Books: Students select and illustrate important vocabulary from the content read.

Pamphlets: Students develop a question/response pamphlet connected to the unit studied. For example, through a study of habitats, students could generate questions about types of habitats and then provide answers to these questions.

Ads/Commercials: Students write ad copy, perhaps for a historical innovation such as the cotton gin. The goal is to include multiple salient historical facts about the invention as well as to write in a lively, enticing manner.

Electronic Resources: Students devise Web sites, personal web pages, or engage in e-mail correspondence, perhaps in the context of a particular historical period being studied.

Whatever the content, writing for authentic purposes is a sure way to engage your students more actively and personally in the subject matter. And that will not only help them learn more, but also help them write better. Have fun with these mini-lessons.

> ### Cat
> Dear Mom,
>
> I think we should get a cat because they make a good pet. A cat is very loving and loyal. Plus it would make me very happy.
>
> We should get a cat because a cat chases mice. Then we would have to keep mice poison in the garage, because the cat would catch it.
>
> Since a cat eats very little we wouldn't have to spend a ton of money on cat food. If you don't want to pay I will.
>
> A cat stays very clean and we wouldn't have to clean it most of the times. Then we wouldn't have to buy shampoo, but if we did I would pay for it.
>
> Thats why we <u>need</u> a cat for a pet.
>
> Sincerely,
> Jennifer
>
> P.S. You are the best mom ever!

This student has learned to compose a persuasive argument, as demonstrated here in a letter to her parents.

Filling out job applications

Skills Focus

Writing persuasive pieces

Organizing writing into a logical order

Making appropriate word choices

Supporting writing with relevant, clearly stated positions

. . . as part of the study of careers in all subjects

Materials & Resources

☆ Photocopies of Job Application form (see Appendix, p. 94), two for each student

Quick Hints

You might extend this exercise by having students design résumés and fill out job applications for different careers related to specific content the class is studying. For example, creative jobs during a unit on westward expansion might include wagon-train leader, cook, teacher, wagon driver, scout; or serious jobs during various science units might include astronaut, geologist, pilot, radiologist.

STEPS

1. In preparation for this lesson, create a list of jobs that will make life easier for you in the classroom and that will, at the same time, provide students with the experience of taking on responsibility. Here is a sampling of possible jobs:

   ☆ Horticulturalist (tends to the plants)
   ☆ Librarian (organizes, advertises, and catalogs books)
   ☆ Resource Manager (organizes and distributes supplies)
   ☆ Environmental Protection Specialist (keeps the room orderly)
   ☆ Human Resources Specialist (troubleshoots minor problems)
   ☆ Primary Teacher's Aide (reads books to younger children)
   ☆ Bookkeeper (marks off homework, carries records to office)

2. Engage the class in a discussion about the jobs that will be offered. Describe the jobs for students, making sure they know what each entails.

3. Using a transparency of the Job Application form (Appendix, p. 94), model for students how you complete the form. As you model, point out and discuss each of the tips listed below. Because drafting and revising are part of the process, include some points in your first draft that you decide you want to change, and model how you revise to create a final, well-crafted application. (We recommend that you make up an additional job for this exercise, one that is not among those you are actually offering, so that students will not be influenced by your choice or the specific information you fill in.)

   ☆ Be straightforward and to the point.
   ☆ Put only the most pertinent information on the application. Write legibly, using your best handwriting.
   ☆ Be as neat as possible since this may be considered a reflection of your work.
   ☆ Work on a draft first so that your final version will be well organized.
   ☆ Think beyond paid positions when experience is called for.

4. Now distribute two photocopies of the Job Application form to each student. Have students fill out the form, following the tips and modeling, and then revise to create a final draft. (Note: Tell students that they each need to fill out a form, even if they do not wish to actually take on a job. Tell them to note their intentions on the back of the form.)

5. Have students turn in their applications. Award jobs based on qualifications and on quality of the way the job application form has been filled out. If you have many qualified applicants for one job, you might consider filling it with several students, on a rotating basis.

Publishing on a web page

EXPLANATION: In this lesson, the traditional research report writing gets a techno-twist that students will enjoy! Most students have likely had a great deal of exposure to the Internet. Why not have them publish in the same format they've enjoyed exploring and take a motivational break from the traditional, conventional report?

Skills Focus

Writing informational pieces

Summarizing and organizing ideas gained from multiple sources

Using word processing and available technology for presentation

Publishing in various formats

. . . as part of the study of maps in social studies

Materials & Resources

☆ Computer with Internet capability (In absence of Internet connection, you can still do this lesson by using publishing software or regular text box features of a word processing program, or by having students draft a template on paper.)

☆ Transparencies of interesting Web site pages you have printed out

☆ Content information to form basis of web page

STEPS

1. Tell students that in this lesson they will have an opportunity to work with a small group or partner to create a unique, new web page. (See note in Materials & Resources: If you have an Internet connection that is convenient and easily available, then the class may engage in the creation of actual web pages; if this is not the case, you can simulate the experience for them via a regular computer publishing program or even using paper templates, and they will still gain experience in the majority of this lesson's skills. Naturally, depending on your situation, you will need to advise the class ahead of time about what their ultimate product will consist of.)

2. Provide students with information about several Web sites that offer reliable informational text on interesting, age-appropriate topics. Here are some suggested Web sites: www.howstuffworks.com, www.enchantedlearning.com, and www.scholastic.com. If you have the capability, visit these sites together as a class by using a computer display that facilitates large-group Internet exploration. If such a setup is not available, explore Web sites via transparencies that you have prepared ahead of the lesson (see Materials & Resources).

3. As you observe these pages, call on students to help you make a list of the features that are most appealing and effective. Among these features might be

   ☆ Graphics/visuals
   ☆ Organization (headings/subheadings)
   ☆ Colors
   ☆ Additional resources offered
   ☆ Easy to read—short, concise
   ☆ Voice used in informational writing

4. Provide students with information that they will incorporate into their own web page. To start, you might give them the information and have them simply translate it to a web page so that their focus is primarily on how best to design the page for clear communication. Later, students could be challenged to do their own research before creating a page. Most content that the class is studying would be appropriate for the research. A sample set of facts that students could use for this model lesson is on page 63.

Quick Hints

Because students are motivated to do better work when they know that others will read what they've written, you might coordinate with other teachers to have their classes review the web pages that your students design.

If you lack the technical skills for web page creation, check out helpful Web sites such as:

www.webmonkey.com,

www.aei.ca/~star/
mywebmaster.htm,

www.itrc.ucf.edu/
conferences/fetc2004/images/
writing.jpg

or enter "creating web pages" on your search engine.

TOPIC: Exploring Maps	
What are some of the major types of maps?	Road maps—help us find places
	Geological maps—show location of natural resources
	Thematic maps—show patterns (i.e., population, rainfall, crops, etc.)
	Topological—show places positioned in relationship to others without correct scale (i.e., subways, trains, buses)
	Meteorological maps—show atmospheric conditions
	Time zone maps—show time zones as they change around the world
What are some useful map terms?	Legend—symbols or colors used to represent items such as airports, parks, cities, capitals
	Projections—mathematical formulas that create images that flatten the Earth and show areas in two dimensions
	Scale—allows reader to translate actual distances based on distances on map
	Indexes—column numbers and letters listed in back of the map book that allow one to locate certain places with precision and ease

5. Once students have the content necessary, set them loose designing their own pages. You might have them work individually, or divide them into pairs. Provide a set of guiding questions, such as those below, to help them as they come up with a design.

☆ What major headings/subheadings will you use?

☆ Which ideas lend themselves to graphics/charts/illustrations?

☆ What special effects can be used for key words and other items that need emphasis?

☆ Where would links for additional information be helpful?

☆ What types of graphics would be helpful and appealing?

☆ How should information be placed on the page?

Writing persuasive letters

EXPLANATION: Students at the intermediate-grade level often hold strong opinions about topics. At the same time, they must learn to back up their opinions with equally strong facts. Writing content-based persuasive letters helps them see that well-structured arguments can make a difference in real-world events.

Skills Focus

Taking notes from almanacs, newspapers, periodicals, and the Internet as informational resources

Writing persuasive letters

. . . *as part of the study of trade agreements among countries*

Materials & Resources

☆ Transparency and photocopies, one for each student, of Persuasive Writing flow chart (see Appendix, p. 92)

☆ Transparency and photocopies, one for each student, of a persuasive letter template (format the same as a standard business letter)

STEPS

Note: Although we have not broken this lesson into parts, it should be considered a multiday lesson. The focus on the first day is on your modeling of how to use the persuasive writing graphic organizer and how to turn this flow chart into a cohesive persuasive argument; the focus on subsequent days is on students' research and writing of their own persuasive letters.

1. Tell students that in this lesson they will have the opportunity to write a letter expressing a strong, personal opinion that is aimed at influencing a powerful person or institution's pending decision. Remind students that this kind of letter is a special form of a business letter, known as a persuasive letter. Review these elements of a persuasive business letter:
   - ☆ Be sure to identify yourself and state your opinion
   - ☆ Use supporting facts and concrete examples
   - ☆ Connect ideas using logic and reasoning
   - ☆ Keep the audience in mind throughout the writing

2. Review as well correct business letter format and required punctuation.

3. Discuss with students the content and information they will be using as the basis for their persuasive letters. In this lesson, the focus is on trade agreements. Discuss the concept of economic interdependence among countries and regions in the past and the present. Invite students to choose a country and to imagine that their country has to make a trade agreement with a different country. They must request an agreement from the leader of that nation regarding a product that their own nation is famous for.

4. Model the process for students as you select the country and product(s) you will use for your sample letter. Examples to stimulate thinking follow:

   U.S.:

denim jeans	oranges	Barbie dolls
tennis shoes	furniture	cars
steel	corn	
peanuts	aircraft	

   OTHER COUNTRIES:

Spain:	Japan:	India:
olives	electronic goods	rugs
olive oil	spices	spices
almonds	cars	fabrics

5. Think aloud further as you decide, based in part on the list on page 64, to persuade the leader of Spain to enter into a trade agreement with the United States involving Nike tennis shoes from the U.S. and olives and olive oils from Spain.

6. Using a transparency of the Persuasive Writing flow chart graphic organizer (Appendix, p. 92) model writing a convincing opinion supported by concrete facts and persuasive elements. Demonstrate for students how you insert key facts for the model letter into the organizer.

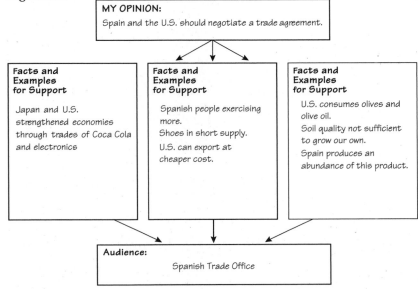

MY OPINION:
Spain and the U.S. should negotiate a trade agreement.

Facts and Examples for Support

Japan and U.S. strengthened economies through trades of Coca Cola and electronics

Facts and Examples for Support

Spanish people exercising more.
Shoes in short supply.
U.S. can export at cheaper cost.

Facts and Examples for Support

U.S. consumes olives and olive oil.
Soil quality not sufficient to grow our own.
Spain produces an abundance of this product.

Audience:
Spanish Trade Office

7. Now model for students how you create a cohesive persuasive letter from the facts and opinions you have sorted out and organized. As you do so, think aloud about the parts of the letter, focusing especially on how you build your persuasive argument from paragraph to paragraph. Point out, too, how you include the correct format of introductory, supporting, and concluding paragraphs, and how you incorporate appropriate transitions. A sample persuasive letter follows:

October 22, 2006
48 G Avenue NW
Washington, DC 20554

Spanish Trade Office
Mr. Michael Perez
2270 Lopez Street
Madrid, Spain

Dear Mr. Perez:

As head of the U.S. Trade Organization, I am aware that our country has grown economically because of the cooperative trade agreements with other countries. We feel strongly that Spain and the U.S. can negotiate an agreement that benefits both parties.

Our citizens only have to remember how Japan agreed to import Coca-Cola and in turn, export electronics. Both products have sustained the economy of each country.

Why not create an analogy of this agreement with the U.S. and Spain? It has recently come to our attention that your citizens are reacting to the health crisis by exercising more. However, the sports shoes necessary for exercise are in short supply. A recent newspaper article illustrates the graveness of this situation with this quote: "When Spanish citizens have to pay $200 for a pair of tennis shoes, then it is time for a change in our leadership." The U.S. can export tennis shoes to Spain, and it will cut your current costs in half.

In turn, our population has developed a fondness for fine cuisine and gourmet cooking. The superior olives and olive oils are in great demand, and our soil does not produce this high-quality product. Spain produces an abundance of these excellent olives and oils and could export these products to the U.S.

It appears to be a perfect trade agreement, where both countries will reap the benefits. We eagerly await your response.

Sincerely,
James Daniel Jones
U. S. Trade Organization

8. Divide the class into small groups and have students discuss plans for their letters. Suggest that they use almanacs, encyclopedias, and other resources for ideas. After determining content, they should complete their own graphic organizers and then write persuasive letters. Circulate among the groups as they work, reminding them as necessary to include strong, fact-based persuasive elements. Check too for correct business letter format, correct paragraphing, and correct spelling.

Writing editorials

STEPS

1. Tell students that in this lesson they will have an opportunity to write an original editorial. Read aloud an editorial from your local paper. Choose one that is brief, straightforward, and easy to grasp.

2. Hold a class discussion about the special characteristics of an editorial. Help students identify the following elements and list them on the chalkboard or a transparency:
   ☆ A strong introduction
   ☆ States the issue clearly
   ☆ Explains the writer's position
   ☆ Presents ideas logically
   ☆ Supports ideas with facts or expert opinions
   ☆ Answers opposing viewpoints
   ☆ Ends with strong argument or a call for action

3. Review with students the content facts they will be using as the basis for their editorials. In this lesson, we focus on the positive and negative aspects of taxation. Discuss historical facts such as the following:

   In the 1700s King George III taxed colonists to help pay for the French and Indian War and to keep the British soldiers in North America. The people became angry. Some colonists began to boycott British goods. Even tax collectors were beaten and their homes destroyed. The Stamp Act led to the Boston Tea Party and eventually to the First Continental Congress.

   After 1868, Reconstruction projects were introduced. Hospitals and schools were built. Roads, bridges, and railroads were repaired. High taxes were placed on land to pay for these projects. These taxes hurt the land owners, forcing some to sell.

   In 1913 President Taft allowed the federal government to tax the people's incomes. This became the 16th Amendment to the Constitution.

   Today, United States citizens have responsibilities, which include taking part in elections, staying informed about current events, helping defend our country, serving on juries, and paying taxes. Congress has the authority to raise money to run the nation. Taxes must be paid if the nation is to run smoothly.

4. Bring the discussion into current times, allowing students time to reflect on their local, state, and federal taxes (food, clothing, gasoline, goods, property, state and federal income taxes, hotels, etc.). Discuss the benefits received from taxes (highway maintenance, fire and police protection, public libraries, state and national parks, public education, etc.). Discuss the negatives

---

EXPLANATION: As students mature, they are increasingly able to sort out their opinions and take a pro or con stance about an issue. Having the opportunity to write an editorial not only gives them a chance to express their opinions, but allows them to put their thoughts into writing in a real-life context.

Skills Focus

Finding ideas for stories and descriptions in conversation with others

Brainstorming to select ideas and information

Planning writing with details, using graphic organizers, notes, etc.

Writing an editorial

. . . as part of the study of the role of the government in levying taxes

Materials & Resources

☆ Simple editorial from your local newspaper

☆ Researched facts about a content area topic

---

associated with taxes (large percentage of income withheld, some projects paid for with taxes only benefit a few people, property owners heavily taxed in some states, etc.).

5. On a transparency, model the process of writing an editorial. As you write, think aloud about the introduction, ideas, facts, and ending and refer to the important elements in the checklist above. Below is a sample editorial:

> Taxes…love 'em or hate 'em. As early as the 1700s the people of the United States paid taxes to a governing body. Many people strongly oppose taxes, but many feel that they are necessary for a civilized quality of life. In a recent issue of *USA Today* in an article titled, "Where Do Our Taxes Go?" the reporter reminded us of the many benefits we receive from the taxes we pay. With respect to our own town, we reflect on the newly paved road that is the entrance to one of our most populated neighborhoods, the state funded Palmetto Fellows Scholarships that many town children receive, books always available for borrowing from the public library, and the S.C. State Park where many townsfolk enjoy a picnic. These many benefits are supported by our tax dollars. Yes, many times we feel that taxes are unfair, but it is our responsibility as United States citizens to continue to pay our share. We must work tirelessly to see that our elected officials are using our taxes wisely.

6. Encourage small groups to reflect on and further consider the whole-class discussion of taxation. Have students sort out their opinions and stances, perhaps making use of a t-chart (see lesson on page 28) to help them as they take notes and figure out their positions.

7. Finally, have students write their own editorials. Each small group might generate one editorial or you might challenge students to each write their own. Afterward, have volunteers read aloud and share their editorials with the class.

8. Post a display chart, "Checklist for an Editorial," of the points listed in Step 2. Consider, as well, making a photocopied version for each student. After writing their editorials, students can check off their work against the criteria.

Quick Hints

Invite students to write "historical" editorials—what would a Tory-supported newspaper have written about King George's taxes versus a newspaper run by the colonists? Or, in a science context, challenge students to write editorials about past controversies such as whether hospitals should take measures against the invisible germs that many people didn't believe even existed, and so on.

Three-Part Lesson: Writing and Giving a Speech
Part 1: Planning and organizing

EXPLANATION: Oral speaking involves a set of important subskills, each of which is valuable for students to acquire. In the first part of this multipart lesson, students map out information and organize it according to the elements of an effective speech.

Skills Focus

Planning writing with details using graphic organizers

Taking notes from almanacs, newspapers, periodicals, and the Internet as informational resources

Analyzing published examples as models for writing

. . . as part of the study of historical settlements and the Jamestown colony

Materials & Resources

☆ Relevant content facts and data

☆ Prepared transparency of the Speech Organizer chart (see p. 70)

☆ Photocopies, one for each student, of the Speech Organizer chart (see p. 70)

☆ Resources such as the following: www.pbs.org/greatspeeches/timeline/ www.americanrhetoric.com/speechbank.htm www.historyplace.com/speeches/previous.htm www.historychannel.com/speeches/

STEPS

1. Discuss with the class the elements of a good speech. Help students identify the following elements and list them on the chalkboard or a transparency:
   ☆ Appropriate to the audience
   ☆ Remains focused on purpose
   ☆ Catches the readers' or audiences' attention
   ☆ States opinions
   ☆ Groups reasons logically
   ☆ Elaborates on reasons with facts
   ☆ Ends with a call to action
   ☆ Uses correct grammar
   ☆ Uses correct spelling, usage, and mechanics

2. Tell students that in this multipart lesson they will have the opportunity to first plan and organize and then write and present an original speech based on historical facts. Review with students the content facts they will be using as the basis for their speeches. In this lesson, we focus on John Smith's efforts to save Jamestown. Discuss historical facts such as the following:

Facts About the Colony of Jamestown

Business people who formed the Virginia Company of London founded the English colony of Jamestown, Virginia, in 1607. Their purpose was to make a profit by building a trading post and colony in North America. Other individuals came to look for gold.

The settlement environment included bad water, wet land, mosquitoes, and disease. The settlers were always in danger of an Indian attack because they took their land and destroyed their crops. Many colonists died from diseases, war, and starvation. No one bothered to plant or gather food for the winter.

When Captain John Smith became the leader of Jamestown, he saved the colony. Captain Smith was a strong and firm leader. The environment and the relationships among the people changed when he required that every colonist must work in order to eat. Shelters were built, gardens were planted, and fences were erected for protection. John Smith made peace with Chief Powhatan who was the leader of an Indian confederation.

The colony survived as the colonists cooperated with and depended on each other for help. Eventually, growing and selling tobacco became an important and profitable business for Jamestown.

☆ Copeland, Lamm, and McKenna. *The World's Great Speeches*. Dover Publishers, 4th edition, 1999.

☆ Macarthur, B. *The Penguin Book of Twentieth Century Speeches*. Penguin USA, 2000.

Quick Hints

Allow students to listen to recordings, CDs, and videotapes highlighting famous speeches, such as those of Nathan Hale, Benedict Arnold, Patrick Henry, Martin Luther King, Jr., and U.S. presidents. Many are available through www.pbs.org /teachersource/search.

3. Model for students how you plan and organize your own speech. Explain that it's a good idea to map out the major elements of a speech ahead of writing. On a transparency, present the Speech Organizer chart, thinking aloud as you decide on and fill in the key elements. (You can use a blank version of the chart below as a model for preparing both the transparency and for photocopies.) A sample, completed chart follows:

Determine audience	the Jamestown colonists
Purpose	to convince the colonists to work together to save Jamestown
Attention getter	strong feelings
Opinion	by cooperating, the settlement can survive
Reasons	provide ample food by planting and cultivating gardens, hunting and fishing for food keep water sources clean by proper care of living sites make friends with the Indians by not taking their land or destroying their crops
Call to action	Ask settlers to work in groups to carry out the requests.

4. Divide the class into pairs or small groups. Distribute a photocopy of the Speech Organizer to each pair or group. Provide published speeches for the groups to analyze for good speech elements. See Materials & Resources for a list of possible resources.

5. Have partners or groups use trade books, biographies, encyclopedias, and online resources to further research and then discuss the targeted historical character. For this lesson, each group could report one leadership characteristic about John Smith to the whole class. These characteristics can set the tone for the speeches. (Possible characteristics: honesty, friendship, loyalty, dependability, etc.) Based on their examination of famous speeches and their further research, have groups fill in their Speech Organizer charts.

Three-Part Lesson: Writing and Giving a Speech
Parts 2 and 3: **Writing and giving the speech**

EXPLANATION: Oral speaking involves a set of important subskills, each of which is valuable for students to acquire. In the latter two parts of this multipart lesson, students write original speeches and have the opportunity to present them orally to the class.

Skills Focus

Taking notes from almanacs, newspapers, periodicals, and the Internet as informational resources

Writing persuasive pieces about events, books, issues, and experiences

Sharing writing orally with others

. . . as part of the study of historical settlements and the Jamestown colony

Materials & Resources

☆ Completed Speech Organizer chart from Part 1 of this lesson

Quick Hints

As students listen to a classmate's speech, have them check off the criteria included on the Speech Organizer chart. Follow with small group discussions in which students record specific examples for each criterion.

STEPS (Part 2)

1. Review the Speech Organizer chart that you created with the class in Part 1 of this lesson. Using this completed chart as a guide, model how you write an effective speech. Think aloud about the elements as you write. For instance, point out how you

   ☆ start the speech with an attention getter because the colonists may be indifferent to what John Smith thinks.

   ☆ set the tone by using a leadership characteristic such as friendship. Continue by stating an opinion and providing reasons and facts.

   ☆ end with a call to action.

   A sample speech follows:

   To my friends, businessmen, gold seekers, and farmers…we must band together to save Jamestown or our colony will not survive! Our hard work and hardships should not be in vain.

   We can rescue the starving by planting food that will sustain us through the winter. Hunting for wild boar and wild turkeys will produce the meat that we need to fight off disease. The fish we catch from our rivers, streams, and ocean will provide food for our citizens and fertilizer for our plants.

   Our water sources can be kept cleaner. If each one cleans up his own living space, a difference will result.

   Make peace with the Indians. We should not take their land and crops as our own. We can all live together in this great colony. Stand with me here on this date in 1610 and join your fellow settlers to reach one common goal—survival!

2. Using the checklist in Step 1 of Part 1 of this lesson, model how you evaluate your speech by reviewing each criterion and checking it off.

STEPS (Part 3)

1. Review with students a checklist of effective behaviors for presenting a speech. A sample checklist follows:

   ☆ List main ideas from each paragraph on note cards. Number the cards.

   ☆ Practice by speaking slowly and clearly. Practice in a small group.

   ☆ Make eye contact with the audience.

2. Model for the class an oral presentation of your speech. Invite each pair or group to select one speaker and have that student present the speech orally.

Writing a nonfiction book review

EXPLANATION: This lesson turns the traditional book report into a more exciting, real-life task for students. They are challenged to become book reviewers and to write a thoughtful book review that ends with a "thumbs up" or "thumbs down" recommendation for their peers.

Skills Focus

Writing persuasive pieces (writing a book review to help others decide if they might be interested in reading the book)

Publishing in various formats

. . . *as part of the study of a nonfiction book about the California gold rush*

Materials & Resources

☆ A nonfiction book that you have read ahead of the lesson. Used in this lesson: *The California Gold Rush* by R. Conrad Stein

☆ A variety of additional nonfiction books on topics related to a unit of content area study

STEPS

1. In preparation for this lesson, make available to students a copy of a nonfiction book that relates to a content unit the class is currently studying. Invite them to browse through the book and to become familiar with it before the lesson. For this lesson, we use *The California Gold Rush* by R. Conrad Stein.

2. Ask students if they've ever been influenced by a movie review that they read or heard about before they attended a movie. Tell the class that like movie reviewers, literary critics—or book reviewers—write for newspapers in almost every city in the country and often influence what the public chooses to buy and read. Some of these reviewers write about nonfiction; others specialize in fiction. In today's lesson, students will learn how to write a review of a nonfiction book.

3. Discuss with the class the elements of a good nonfiction book review. Help students identify the following elements and list them on the chalkboard or a transparency:
   ☆ Give author, title, and a brief summary of the book
   ☆ Explain what you think the book's purpose is
   ☆ Support your thoughts with quotations, reasons, and other evidence
   ☆ Show why the book is important to the reader
   ☆ End with a restatement or give a recommendation for the book

4. Hold up the book that you will be reviewing. On a transparency or on the chalkboard, write the words shown in boldface below. Tell students that these are the headings for a nonfiction book review outline, formed from the elements list you have brainstormed with the class. Model how you fill in this outline, thinking aloud about the book as you do so. A sample completed outline follows:

NONFICTION BOOK REVIEW OUTLINE

Author, title:
The California Gold Rush by R. Conrad Stein

Summary points:
Indians, the '49ers, the railroads, law and order, the economy

Purpose:
To provide a historical account of the gold rush in 1849

Support:
Facts about the gold rush
Escalating prices (iron pans example)
Entrepreneurs (Levi Strauss)

Why book is important to the reader:
To satisfy reading about this period in history—the Wild West

Ending:
Recommendation for reading? Yes: good pictures and illustrations, excellent personal stories

5. Using a transparency, model how you write the book review. Refer to the outline of the elements as you write. A sample book review follows:

A Review of <u>The California Gold Rush</u>

If you like to read about the Wild West, then you will surely want to read <u>The California Gold Rush</u> by R. Conrad Stein. The author provides a historical account of the gold rush in 1849 and how the '49ers, the Indians, the railroads, the economy, and law and order were affected.

The author takes you on a "brief but furious" trip through this period of history. Along the way you learn of John Sutter, Joe Dye, Philip Armour, and Levi Strauss and their personal stories of defeat and success. You will learn about the money made by business owners because of the rush of thousands that established instant communities. A businessman in one "boomtown" bought up all the iron pans used in gold mining for 20 cents apiece and sold them for $8 apiece. Levi Strauss began to make pants for the miners out of tough denim. These jeans are still popular today. Men fought over how to divide the gold fairly, and an average of two murders a day took place at the height of the rush.

Mr. Stein included many pictures, illustrations, and a glossary and time line to offer a clear image of this time. Because of these elements and the excellent personal stories, I would hope that you would read this book.

6. To extend this lesson, provide students with a wide array of nonfiction books on current content area studies. Have each student select a book and use the outline to write a book review.

Coming to America: Ellis Island
A Model Unit of Integrated Instruction

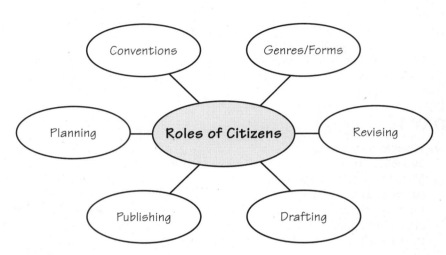

This model unit blends writing, reading, and one content area—social studies—in an extended and fully developed unit that illustrates thorough integration of language arts and content in the classroom. Unlike the briefer lessons in this book, we present here specific content area standards, along with those for language arts.

How can you use this unit? You may wish to use it in its entirety as it fits into your course of study as you teach the roles of citizens. However, if it doesn't fit into your curriculum plan as a single entity, we hope that you'll discover its other benefits. For instance, its individual mini-lessons can be used as templates for designing your own lessons in other disciplines and with other content, just as is the case with the lessons in Sections 1 through 5.

Our greatest hope is that it can serve as a model for you of how to achieve the depth of instruction that we, along with so many other educators, believe is critical. Rather than being "a mile wide and an inch deep," as critics often refer to current curricular designs, it moves far beyond such shallowness, interconnecting many different kinds of skills and encouraging probing, problem solving, and experiential learning.

We hope you will also discover a further distinctive feature as you use this unit. It aims to incorporate a powerful environmental method of writing instruction (Hillocks, 1986) in which process and procedures are taught, where more collaboration occurs among writers, and where more student-directed criteria are included to which writers learn to hold themselves accountable. You'll notice the many checklists that help to establish these criteria. At grades 4–6, we're moving students toward independence as writers, and in this unit, you'll see how we suggest accomplishing this more fully. Teaching students to internalize their own criteria for quality raises the bar, so to speak, on students' writing. The research of Hillocks and Smith contends that this method of writing instruction is, indeed, the most powerful that we can employ in our classrooms.

Within this unit, which extends over a period of approximately 22 days, you'll find thorough integration of social studies and language arts skills, most specifically writing skills. The writing mini-lessons range from basic conventions to a culminating project where students create and produce a Readers' Theater, requiring them to read, write, assimilate information, revise, craft text, edit, and publish. Equally important, though, we hope that the outcome of the unit will be that your students better grasp the true meaning of being a United States citizen. We hope your students will learn from it and that together you and they will enjoy it!

Coming to America: Ellis Island

Days 1 to 13: Immigration Research Report

DAY 1

1. With your students, look at the word *immigrant* and point out its word parts: *im-*, which means "in," and *migrant*, which means "one who moves from one place to another." When people move to one country from another they are referred to as "immigrants" by the people already living in that country. Using the following facts and any others of your choosing, lead students in a discussion about how many people became United States citizens from 1892 to 1914 as immigrants from other countries:

   ☆ Most immigrants (about 90 percent) entered the country through Ellis Island off the coast of New York.

   ☆ Immigrants were of all ages and nationalities.

   ☆ Many of these people were escaping difficult conditions in their native countries.

   ☆ Many were looking for the "streets of gold" they felt the U.S. promised them.

   ☆ Immigrants were not all admitted into the U.S. upon their arrival.

2. You may wish to stimulate discussion with some of these thought-provoking questions:

   ☆ How would the lack of media and technology in the years 1892 to 1914 have made the move to America more uncertain than it would today?

   ☆ In what ways would the move be easier or harder today than in the years 1892 to 1914?

   ☆ With very limited packing space, what kinds of things would they have wanted to carry with them on this journey, knowing that they would never likely return to their native country?

   ☆ Under what conditions would they consider making a permanent move to another country today?

3. After the discussion (which could take place in social studies class or during Writing Workshop), arrange students into cooperative groups. Give each group a sheet of chart paper and a marker. Ask each group to brainstorm a list of questions concerning the migration of people into the U.S. in the years 1892 to 1914 through Ellis Island. Have them list their questions on chart paper.

4. Have each group post their questions on the wall in the classroom, allowing adequate space between the charts for later group work.

Language arts standards in this lesson:

Writing informational pieces

Framing questions to direct research

Generating ideas

Finding ideas for stories and descriptions in pictures and books, magazines, textbooks, the Internet, conversation with others, and newspapers.

DAY 2

1. Let students know that they will be gathering information about the immigrants' experience and will eventually write a paper based on their research.

2. Tell students that they'll be deciding on the three questions they're most curious about from the previous day's brainstorming. These three questions will guide them as they gather some

information. Ask them to pay close attention as you model the thought process involved in narrowing the many questions to only three. Walk around the room and read some questions gathered by the cooperative groups. Include in your Think Aloud comments such as these:

☆ "This question might be too specific to find any information. I'm really curious about it, though. So, I might reword it to be a better research question." **Example:** A question such as: "What was the immigration process like for 12-year-olds?" could be reworded as "What was the immigration process like for children?"

☆ "I'll bet there's a lot of information about a question like this. I might want to narrow this one a little." **Example:** "What were the reasons people wanted to migrate to the U.S.?" might become "What were the most popular reasons people migrated to the U.S.?"

3. After gathering a question or two from each group's chart, further narrow your choices to any three questions you like. (If you wish to use the composition provided in this unit, see Step 4 below for your three questions.)

4. Make a transparency of the Research Report Organizer on page 95 of the Appendix. Write your three final questions in the space provided in the left column.

☆ What were the main reasons for the migration of people into the U.S. during the years 1892 to 1914?

☆ What was the process immigrants went through at Ellis Island?

☆ What were the reasons for turning some people away at Ellis Island?

5. Now tell students they'll have an opportunity to find the three questions that most interest them. (You may wish to instruct students that they cannot choose more than one of your questions to work with. Otherwise, they may not learn to go through the process that you are teaching.) Instruct students to each take a sheet of paper and move about the room in their cooperative groups to copy down interesting questions from the charts. They can gather any number of questions at this point, but they should think about questions that might be too broad, too narrow, or that, for them, are not as interesting as others. Give them about two to three minutes at each chart to think about and copy the questions they like. You might set a timer for this and give a signal for groups to rotate among charts.

6. After students have rotated to all of the charts, have them return to their desks. Let them work independently to decide upon the three questions they're most interested in. Give them a copy of the Research Report Organizer (Appendix, p. 95), which they can use to record their three top questions in the space provided.

DAYS 3–5

1. For the next several days, you'll model the steps necessary to gather good research. To start, put pertinent bibliographical information for your resource in the top horizontal box of the Research Report Organizer. Page numbers can be added as you find information.

2. Use the table of contents of the informational book resource to show students how they can pinpoint desired information without necessarily having to read the entire text. Instruct students to listen carefully to the chapter headings as you read them aloud. If students predict that that section will have information related to the question you're searching to answer, tell them to give you a "thumbs up" sign. If their prediction is that the section heading tells you that there is no information related to the question, they should signal with "thumbs down." When the signal is "thumbs up," stop and read or scan that section. Record your notes in the right-hand column for Question 1.

Language arts standards in this lesson:

Writing informational pieces

Framing questions to direct research

Organizing writing into logical order

Notes about materials: We include one form in the Appendix for information gathering. It allows for the use of only one resource. Other forms allowing for as many as three different resources can be created easily by modifying the one-source form to include additional columns for resources. If you choose to use the latter, you may want to offer students three different types of resources (for example, an information book, the Internet, and an encyclopedia) to familiarize them with different kinds of research. For this lesson, we've used the one-resource form and an informational book that has chapter headings: . . . If Your Name Was Changed at Ellis Island.

Language arts standards in this lesson:

Planning writing with details, using lists, graphic organizers, notes and logs, outlines, conceptual maps, learning logs, and time lines

Taking notes by identifying main ideas, evaluating relevancy, and paraphrasing information in resource materials

3. Repeat this process for your next two questions: Pinpoint the specific information, read the information, paraphrase the important and interesting facts, and write them in phrases in the appropriate box in the Research Report Organizer. Point out to students that the boxes on the form are deliberately small. Because the researcher is limited in space, he or she can use only key words and phrases—not sentences—and must be selective about what is recorded. (As well, the small space discourages students from copying directly from the text.) See the completed version of the teacher's model, Figure 1 below.

4. Note that if you are using a three-resource form, you'll need to alert students that not all resources may answer all of their questions. Allow them some "free spaces." You may, however, need to caution them that you don't expect too many "free spaces" or you'll need to revisit their sources with them.

> Taking notes from authoritative sources
>
> Locating information by using tables of contents, prefaces, appendixes, citations, endnotes, and bibliographic references
>
> Using almanacs, newspapers, periodicals, and the Internet as informational resources
>
> Writing informational pieces
>
> Documenting sources for a bibliography

Figure 1: Research Report Organizer (One-Source) for Ellis Island Report

Topic: Ellis Island Title:	Source #1 . . . If Your Name Was Changed at Ellis Island Ellen Levine Scholastic, NY: 1993, pp. 12–16, 35–44, 45–48.
Question #1: What were the reasons that most of the immigrants came to the U.S. during 1892 to 1914?	pp. 12–15 ☆ Ireland—famine due to diseased potato crops; two million starved ☆ Sweden—famine ☆ Russian Jews—religious pogroms ☆ Turkey—deadly flu epidemic ☆ Promise of better life: land, money
Question #2: What was the process immigrants went through at Ellis Island?	pp. 35–51 ☆ Climbing stairs of Great Hall was test ☆ Three-minute exam at top of stairs: skin, scalp, throat, hands, eyes ☆ Marked with chalk if something found ☆ Some put in hospitals or held ☆ Legal inspection: 20–30 questions ☆ Then sent to ferry to Manhattan
Question #3: What were the reasons for turning some people away at Ellis Island?	pp. 50–52 ☆ Physical illnesses ☆ Mental illnesses ☆ Responses to legal questions ☆ Held if not enough money/resources ☆ Many errors made: language barriers, misdiagnosis, too hurried

DAY 6

1. Now you'll start translating your Research Report Organizer into a draft research paper. The organizer will make this process so much easier than students usually find this process! For research reports, writers usually begin by laying out what they're going to report in their paper. The top box in the right-hand column of the organizer combined with the three questions in the left-hand column (see Figure 1), already incorporate all this information; students need simply to turn that information into a good paragraph.

2. Let students know that there are numerous styles they might consider to start their reports. Usually the first sentence or paragraph of informational writing accomplishes one of two things or a combination of these:

   ☆ States the topic and defines or describes it

   ☆ Provides a hook for the reader (Clue: Present some of the most interesting facts from your research to accomplish this hook; create some mystery about the subject or make a personal connection with the reader.)

3. Model a beginning paragraph based on each of these styles and see which one you and the students like best. Following are two sample paragraphs:

   States the topic and defines or describes it:

   > Ellis Island was a gateway into the U.S. for millions of people between 1892 and 1914. Who were these people and why did they come? Why were some of these hopeful people turned away at Ellis Island? These are the interesting questions that will guide us as we explore the answers.

   Provides a hook for the reader:

   > "Pack a shovel for your trip because you'll be shoveling gold from the streets!" This was just one of the dreams that led millions of people to an unfamiliar land during the years from 1892 to 1914. What was this land of the free and home of the brave? Who were these people and why did they risk their lives? Could they make a journey only to be turned away? Let's find out!

4. Choose a lead paragraph for your composition based on what you like best and let students start working on their beginning sentences.

> **Language arts standards in this lesson:**
>
> Planning writing with details, using lists, graphic organizers, notes and logs, outlines, conceptual maps, learning logs, and time lines
>
> Writing effective beginning

> *Notes about materials:*
> *If possible, try to use two overhead projectors for the next few days—one for the graphic organizer and information; one for drafting the research paper.*

DAY 7

1. Today you're ready to write paragraph two of your draft. You'll use the second horizontal row of your Research Report Organizer. (See Figure 1.)
   Note: If you're using a research form for two to three resources, review the notes you've made. If there is any contradictory information, you'll want to show students how to consider the most reliable source—some Internet sites, of course, may not offer thoroughly researched information—or do further research to confirm the most accurate information.

2. Let students know that all of the information in this paragraph should relate to the question they formulated. First, you'll need to synthesize your notes and put them into sentence form on paper. Be sure that students are aware that this is your first draft, and that there will be opportunities to revise. Below is a sample second paragraph:

   > People immigrated to the United States for many reasons around the turn of the 20th century. Some came because of natural disasters. In Ireland, for example, two million people starved to death during the potato famine. Sweden also was suffering from a famine. They had heard that in America they not only could get bread, but butter as well. Many Russian Jews came to America because of the religious massacres or pogroms. The people of Turkey were trying to escape a deadly flu epidemic. For all, America promised a better, wealthier, healthier, and happier life.

3. Now students can continue to work on their lead paragraph and second paragraph.

> **Language arts standards in this lesson:**
>
> Planning writing with details, using lists, graphic organizers, notes and logs, outlines, conceptual maps, learning logs, and time lines
>
> Writing effective middle
>
> Writing pieces with multiple paragraphs (categorize ideas appropriately; include supporting paragraphs)

DAYS 8–9

1. Using the Research Report Organizer, follow the same procedure for the next two paragraphs (Paragraphs 3 and 4) of your report. These paragraphs are based on Questions 2 and 3 and the corresponding information on your organizer. (See Figure 1.) Below are two sample paragraphs:

Paragraph 3, based on Question 2 and corresponding information:

Immigrants had to pass a number of tests at Ellis Island to be processed into the United States. The first of these was to demonstrate that they were healthy enough to walk up the stairs of the Great Hall. Doctors watched them for signs of disabilities. Once they reached the top of the stairs, they were given a three-minute examination of their skin, scalp, throat, hands, and eyes. If they showed any signs of weakness or illness at this point, the doctors put a code on their clothes with chalk. The last test was an interview of 20–30 legal questions.

Paragraph 4, based on Question 3 and corresponding information:

After the numerous tests, the hopeful immigrants could be sent to the ferry for their short trip to Manhattan, held in hospitals, or something worse. After weeks of travel to America, these people could be sent back to their native countries. America did not want the same diseases that had killed millions in other countries. So, those people who were thought to carry diseases were sent back. People with serious mental problems were also turned away. If legal questions made the officials think that the immigrants could not support themselves or were not entitled to own land, they were often sent back. There were many reasons that mistakes were made, and many people were turned away in error.

2. Encourage students to draw from their organizers to draft their third and fourth paragraphs.

> **Language arts standards in this lesson:**
>
> Planning writing with details, using lists, graphic organizers, notes and logs, outlines, conceptual maps, learning logs, and time lines
>
> Writing effective middle
>
> Writing pieces with multiple paragraphs (categorize ideas appropriately; include supporting paragraphs)

DAY 10

1. Now you're ready to write the final paragraph of your first draft. This paragraph usually serves as a summary or a way of "telling them what you've told them." Just as with beginning sentences, there are different styles to consider for endings, for example:

   ☆ Leaving the reader with some of your own reflections on what you've researched and written

   ☆ Merely summarizing the main ideas in the composition

   ☆ Suggesting further thoughts for the reader to consider, often connecting the text to the reader's own life

2. Return to the box at the top of your Research Report Organizer and the three questions (Figure 1) to create your final paragraph. Model for students how you experiment with each of these styles and approaches. Write different paragraphs, such as the following:

Leaving the reader with some of your own reflections of what you've researched and written:

Although the decision to come to America may have been a difficult one for the immigrants, what lay ahead of them was equally difficult. They arrived like cattle on a ship. They were herded onto Ellis Island when they arrived. They were examined like cattle and sorted according to tests given to them hurriedly. Their fate often depended upon the whim of one individual's mood or judgment. The desire for these people to become American citizens had to be greater than most American citizens today can realize.

(In the above model paragraph, point out that you've used a simile that makes it easier for the reader to visualize the masses of immigrants—comparing them to cattle.)

> **Language arts standards in this lesson:**
>
> Planning writing with details, using lists, graphic organizers, notes and logs, outlines, conceptual maps, learning logs, and time lines
>
> Writing effective ending
>
> Writing pieces with multiple paragraphs (categorize ideas appropriately; write a concluding paragraph that summarizes points; engage the interest of the reader)
>
> Forming imagery (similes)

Merely summarizing the main ideas in the composition:

> Therefore, immigrants came to America for so many different reasons but, generally, to find better lives for themselves. The tests they endured at Ellis Island were only a few of the many they had to endure to live in this new country. There were some, however, who left Ellis Island rejected and sad to return after many trials to their own native countries never to know the freedom they desperately wanted in America.

Suggesting further thoughts for the reader to consider, often connecting the text to the reader's own life:

> Can you even imagine the fear and hope of the people who left their home countries with few belongings for life in a place they had only heard stories about? How frightened they must have been! At every step through Ellis Island, they didn't know whether they might say or do something that would send them back to the country they had left behind. What do you think would make you go through an ordeal like these immigrants?

3. Read each of these model paragraphs with your students and decide on the one that you like best. Add it to your draft.

4. Now have students tackle writing endings for their informational pieces, considering the different styles and approaches they have learned.

DAY 11

1. Tell students that you've decided to breathe a little more life into your research paper. One way to do that is to include direct quotations. Quotes from people who actually experienced Ellis Island as immigrants would be particularly interesting. Books that contain first-person accounts are a good source for such quotations. One of our favorites is *I Was Dreaming to Come to America: Memories from Ellis Island Oral History Project,* by Veronica Lawlor, which includes many direct quotations from immigrants.

2. Many Web sites post interviews with immigrants, offering a firsthand perspective and a great opportunity to show students how to incorporate such dialogue into their research. If you have this technology available, use your classroom computer to bring up one of the many Web sites that offer first-person interviews and narratives from immigrants. (Suggested for this lesson is http://teacher.scholastic.com/activities/immigration/tour.) Listen for dialogue that pertains to the questions you've included in your paper. With the computer, it's easy to replay excerpts, allowing you to copy good quotations you might use.

> **Language arts standards in this lesson:**
>
> Planning writing with details, using lists, graphic organizers, notes and logs, outlines, conceptual maps, learning logs, and time lines
>
> Writing pieces with multiple paragraphs (categorize ideas appropriately; include supporting paragraphs; engage the reader)
>
> Using quotation marks in conversation

3. Copy down relevant quotations on separate index cards or on large sticky notes. Be sure to add any citations available. Sample index cards, based on interviews from the Scholastic Web site, follow:

> "We heard a tremendous rumble that got louder and louder and louder. My father and I got dressed, and we ran to the deck. There were people of all denominations...some on their knees making the sign of the cross, Jews in prayer shawls...as we were passing the Statue of Liberty. It was a great sight."
>
> Lawrence Meinwald, Polish immigrant, at the age of 6 in 1920.
> http://teacher.scholastic.com/activities/immigration/tour

"My father had cut his face shaving. They put a white chalk on his lapel. As the line progressed at one point, they pulled him out of the line. Mother started to plead and cry."

Lawrence Meinwald, Polish immigrant, at the age of 6 in 1920.

http://teacher.scholastic.com/activities/ immigration/tour

"I remember my mother saying 'So this is America.' My father said to my mother, 'You're in America now and you have nothing to be afraid of…nothing at all.'"

Estelle Belford, Romanian immigrant, at the age of 5 in 1905.

http://teacher.scholastic.com/activities/immigration /tour

DAY 12

1. Incorporate some of the quotations you gathered from the previous day's lesson. Suggest to students that quotations can be used at different places in a composition—they make good beginnings to grab a reader's attention and good endings as well. They can also be used to illustrate any of the topic sentences— or topic questions—in the Ellis Island draft.

2. Hand out to several different students the index cards containing the quotations from the previous day's lesson. Then call on one of those students to read aloud the quotation on his or her card. Skim over your written composition to see if there is a logical place to incorporate it. If you decide to use it, tape the card in the margin of the paper closest to the point where you'll want to use it. Place an asterisk at the point where you might include the quotation.

3. Continue having students read out the quotation on their card and hunting for places to use them. Not all quotations have to be used. Use only the ones that you feel will liven up your text.

4. Model the specifics of how commas and quotation marks are used. Here are some reminders:

   ☆ In writing the usual exchange of dialogue, the paragraph changes with each speaker. (This may not apply to this composition since it's not likely to involve an exchange of dialogue.)

   ☆ Use only one set of quotation marks when you're quoting more than one sentence from the same source and when the quoted sentences run continuously.

   ☆ Commas and periods go inside quotation marks. Semicolons and colons go outside quotation marks.

5. If quotations are spliced together, you may also need to demonstrate how an ellipsis is used. Inform students that an ellipsis is used to show that some unnecessary words have been omitted from the original text. Tell them to be sure that what is omitted doesn't change the meaning of the sentence. For example:

   "My father had cut his face shaving. They put a white chalk on his lapel. As the line progressed at one point, they pulled him out of the line. Mother started to plead and cry."

   is written as

   "My father had cut his face shaving. They put a white chalk on his lapel…they pulled him out of the line. Mother started to plead and cry."

6. Below is an example of how one of the quotations could be incorporated into the draft on Ellis Island. The first version of the paragraph is rewritten to include the Meinwald quotation shown at the top of this page.

   First version:

   After the numerous tests, the hopeful immigrants could be sent to the ferry for their short trip to Manhattan, held in hospitals, or something worse. After weeks of travel to America, these people could be sent back to their native countries. America did not want the same diseases that had killed millions in other countries. So, those people who were thought to carry

Language arts standards in this lesson:

Writing pieces with multiple paragraphs (categorize ideas appropriately; include supporting paragraphs)

Using commas in direct quotations

Using quotation marks in conversation

Using ellipses appropriately

Revising writing for meaning, clarity, and focus (adding dialogue to engage reader)

diseases were sent back. People with mental problems were also turned away. If legal questions made the officials think that the immigrants could not support themselves or were not entitled to own land, they were often sent back. There were many reasons that mistakes were made, and many people were turned away in error.

The rewritten paragraph:

After the numerous tests, the hopeful immigrants could be sent to the ferry for their short trip to Manhattan, held in hospitals, or something worse. After weeks of travel to America, these people could be sent back to their native countries. America did not want the same diseases that had killed millions in other countries. So, those people who were thought to carry diseases were sent back. People with mental problems were also turned away. If legal questions made the officials think that the immigrants could not support themselves or were not entitled to own land, they were often sent back. There were many reasons that mistakes were made, and many people were turned away in error. Polish immigrant Lawrence Meinwald, who was 6 years old when he immigrated through Ellis Island, remembers, "My father had cut his face shaving. They put a white chalk on his lapel. As the line progressed at one point, they pulled him out of the line. Mother started to plead and cry."

(You may decide that this paragraph is too long. It can easily be divided into two paragraphs, starting at "There were many reasons…")

DAY 13 ....

1. Once you've finished your composition, have students help you apply the following checklist to do your final editing. Encourage them to offer constructive feedback.

   ___There is a strong introductory paragraph that clearly states the topic and the guiding questions.

   ___The research I included has adequately addressed all guiding questions.

   ___There is a strong sense of closure to my research paper.

   ___I have paraphrased my research.

   ___I have checked for correct use of commas.

   ___I have used quotation marks correctly.

   ___My writing has stayed focused through all paragraphs.

2. Use appropriate resources during your editing: thesaurus, dictionary, and others.

3. Finally, instruct students to edit their own reports, following the guidelines and procedures you have modeled.

> **Language arts standards in this lesson:**
>
> Revising writing for meaning, clarity, and focus
>
> Editing writing for correctness, meaning, and clarity
>
> Using appropriate references when editing
>
> Using a simple checklist for revising and editing
>
> Responding in constructive ways to others' writing

Coming to America: Ellis Island
....
Day 14: **Lady Liberty Teaches Symbolism**

DAY 14 ....

1. Show students a picture of the Statue of Liberty. (Many pictures can be found on the Internet.) Tell them that Frederic Auguste Bartholdi used many symbols in the statue he created. These symbols are objects or elements that represent ideas.

2. Divide the class into cooperative groups. Challenge them to discuss, research, and figure out what the various elements of the statue symbolize. In the list below, each element is shown in boldface type; the idea symbolized by an element is in regular type. (Note: The list shown here is already sorted out.)

Points on the headgear
Heaven's rays shining over the world

Torch
Enlightening the way to freedom

Broken shackles around feet	**Tablet**
Freedom from tyranny	Law and order
25 windows around head	**Date inscribed on the tablet**
Seas and continents of the world	Declaration of independence from Britain
Flowing robe	**Upraised foot**
Ancient goddess of liberty	Leading the way to freedom

3. Now, explain to students that writers often use symbols to represent ideas. The symbols and what they stand for may be more abstract than is the case in the Statue of Liberty. Tell students that symbolism is a writing element that assumes that readers are thinkers and that they don't need to be told everything outright. Share with students a published text passage containing symbolism or model an attempt of your own, such as the one below. Have students discuss the passage and identify both the symbol and what it represents.

> Breshna had long struggled with whether she should leave her much beloved country of Russia. Her decision was made one morning as she sat at the kitchen table staring at an apple on the cabinet. Although it appeared to be shiny and delicious, a black spot had developed on one side. How deep was the rot? How long would it take until the bad had consumed the good? And then she knew in an instant what she would do.

4. Symbolism in writing demands that readers be thoughtful and aware as they read. Challenge your students to challenge their own readers—have them compose paragraphs that incorporate symbolism and read these aloud to partners. The partner's task is to identify both the symbol and what it stands for.

> **Language arts standards in this lesson:**
>
> Writing pieces with multiple paragraphs (categorize ideas appropriately; include supporting paragraphs)
>
> Using commas in direct quotations
>
> Using quotation marks in conversation
>
> Using ellipses appropriately
>
> Revising writing for meaning, clarity, and focus (adding material to engage reader)
>
> Forming imagery (symbolism)

Coming to America: Ellis Island

Days 15–19: Journaling to a New Country

DAY 15

1. Let students know that they'll be using their new and increasing knowledge about the Ellis Island experience to write a short version of historical fiction in the form of journal entries.

2. Based on research done previously in this unit, make a list with students of native countries and a reason associated with each for migration to America. For example:

- ☆ Ireland—famine due to diseased potato crops
- ☆ Sweden—famine
- ☆ Russian Jews—religious persecution
- ☆ Turkey—deadly flu epidemic

> **Language arts standards in this lesson:**
>
> Finding ideas for stories and descriptions in pictures and books, magazines, textbooks, Internet, conversation with others, and newspapers.
>
> Brainstorming to select ideas and information
>
> Planning writing with details, using lists, etc.

3. Use this list to select and develop a character who will write the journal entries that you model for students as part of this lesson. Consider some of the questions that must be answered to develop a character. Think aloud as you make notes. Below are some of the things you might need to consider to begin writing your historical fiction journal. (If you're using the sample journal prepared, you'll need to use responses appropriate to the content as indicated in parentheses below.)

- ☆ What name can you give your character that's appropriate to the country you've chosen? (Sarah is an Irish name.)
- ☆ What age would you like your character to be? (For married mothers, you might say that you'd like the character to be similar in age and family situation to your own.)

☆ Will your character be traveling with a family? If so, what is his or her situation? (Again, you may want the situation to be similar to your own—something you can identify with.)

☆ What is the reason your character is writing in a journal? (For someone who is sequestered on a ship for a long period of time with hundreds of other people, a journal could be a great outlet!)

☆ How is your character writing in a journal when materials of all kinds are limited on the voyage to America? (The sample journal explains that a water-damaged book is being used as the journal.)

DAY 16

1. Remind students that a journal allows a writer to share personal feelings and thoughts and to speak with less formality. Remind them, too, that like all historical fiction, their journal entries need to be realistic and must utilize factual information.

2. Below is a model entry you might write for your students. (Note that the underlining, numbering, and circles are relevant to Day 17 and Day 19 lessons.)

3. Call attention to the two examples of interjections used on lines 9 and 18. Explain that these are expressions of surprise that don't have sentence structure but that are often punctuated like sentences.

> **Language arts standards in this lesson:**
>
> Writing pieces with multiple paragraphs (categorize ideas appropriately; include supporting paragraphs)
>
> Using parts of speech correctly (interjections)
>
> Writing in response to what is read and written, using a variety of formats across the curriculum
>
> Writing in learning logs and journals to discover, develop, and refine ideas, including other curriculum areas
>
> Writing a friendly letter

1	May 18, 1902
2	Dear Diary,
3	My name's Sarah, and I'm writing from a storm-tossed ship that has been home
4	to my family now for two weeks. I'm beginning to wonder how far this storm has allowed
5	us to move during all this time. The ship's crew tells us that they've never sailed in weather
6	so stormy for such a long time.
7	My husband, Henry, and I, along with our two young children, inhabit about six
8	square feet during the worst of the weather. For the brief times that the weather has settled,
9	we've dashed up to the deck of the ship, hungry for some breaths of fresh air. Oh, my! The
10	air in our space feels drained of oxygen and thick with the unpleasant smells of seasickness
11	and depression.
12	The ship took on water badly one night. The books that had been our solace were stripped
13	of their words—ink evaporating as the books dried. The silver lining of that damage was that
14	I'm using one of those books now as my journal, replacing the faded words of world-famous poets
15	and authors with my own primitive writing. My friend, I hope that sharing with you will help me
16	keep my sanity on this voyage.
17	I know you're curious about why we're here. Why would we leave our once beloved country of
18	Ireland with all of its vast beauty to travel like cattle to a land we've never seen? Oh! It's quite
19	a story, but you'll have to wait until tomorrow. Just as I've begun, Jamie appears ready for bed,
20	and I must sing him to sleep. Until tomorrow . . .
21	Your new friend,
22	Sarah

DAY 17

1. Reread the previous day's entry and comment that you feel something about the speaker's voice isn't quite consistent with the era and with what you've been reading about this era. Think aloud as you focus on the numerous contractions that you've used. Explain that these make the writer's voice sound less formal than was typically true of adults at the turn of the century.

2. Ask students to help you identify all of the contractions in your piece. (Refer to the underlined material.) As you identify each, provide explanation of contractions if your students need such review. Then, invite students to help you make decisions about whether some or all the contractions should be omitted and replaced to make the voice consistent with the time period and the character.

3. Now, it's time for students to work on their own journal entries. Alert them that whatever they choose to write today needs to be able to be shared with the class as a part of tomorrow's lesson.

> **Language arts standards in this lesson:**
>
> Organizing writing into a logical order (choose point-of-view based on purpose, audience, length and format requirements)
>
> Writing pieces with multiple paragraphs (categorize ideas appropriately; include supporting paragraphs)
>
> Writing narratives that describe and explain familiar objects, events, and experiences
>
> Revising writing for meaning, clarity, and focus (add and delete)
>
> Using apostrophes in contractions
>
> Responding in constructive ways to others' writings

DAY 18

1. Today you'll share with your students a great peer revision technique. Display your journal entry on the overhead projector and read it aloud to the class.

2. Ask students to think of questions about what you've written and about what you haven't had the opportunity to write yet. What piques their curiosity about the family you've created? Give two sticky notes to each student. Have students each brainstorm one to two discussion questions and write these questions on the sticky notes.

3. Collect the notes and read through them. If any of them pertain to what you've written, stick them directly on the transparency at the relevant spot in your journal entry. Offer rationale about whether you feel that question gets at information that your readers need and/or would make your writing more interesting.

4. If the questions you're offered don't pertain to what you've written so far, tell students that you'll put the notes aside and consider them as you write. They might help you arrive at valuable details that will greatly enhance your story.

5. Divide the class into cooperative groups of four students. Give each student in a group six to eight sticky notes, all of one color. Thus, student #1 will have all green, student #2 all blue, student #3 all yellow, and so on.

6. Tell each student to take out the first journal entry they've written and pass it to the person on the right. Each person in the group will read a buddy's paper and write one to two questions about the story so far, stick it to the author's paper, and then pass it on to the person to their right. That person in turn will read the same paper, write a question or two, put the sticky notes on the paper, and pass it on to the next person. The papers will circulate among the three readers and will then return to the author.

7. Once papers have been returned to their owners, instruct the owners to read all of the questions generated by their peers and follow the procedure described on the next page.

> **Language arts standards in this lesson:**
>
> Revising writing for meaning, clarity, and focus (add and delete)
>
> Responding in constructive ways to others' writings

> *Notes about materials:*
> *four different colors of sticky-note pads (Each student will need six to eight sheets of one color.)*

☆ Decide if the question is one that would make the journal more interesting.

☆ If not, the writer may discard it.

☆ If the question is a "keeper" and it is immediately relevant, the writer should put it right to use to improve what he or she has already written.

☆ If the answer doesn't help the part already written, the writer should set it aside on his/her desk or writing folder to consider adding to subsequent writing.

8. Note that this approach can be used on many occasions to offer guidance for revisions in writing.

DAY 19

1. Use your journal entry to model for students the many uses of the comma. Project a transparency of the entry and read it aloud. As you read, comment about the numerous commas that you've included. Then, tell students that there is even more to know about the effective use of commas.

> **Language arts standard in this lesson:**
>
> Using commas appropriately (in direct quotations; with appositives; before conjunctions; in dates; in salutation and closing of letter)

2. Number the lines of your piece in the margin.

3. Invite different students to come up to the overhead projector and trace over the commas in each paragraph with a colored transparency pen.

4. Ask students to take out a sheet of lined paper and draw a line down the page about one to two inches from the left margin. Have them include headings like those shown in the chart below.

5. To the left of the line they've drawn, have them write the line number for each comma. If lines have more than one comma, they should list the line number again for each comma. To the right, have them take notes on the use of the comma as you talk about them. You might make this interactive, seeing what students already know about comma usage. If many of these uses are new to them, they won't absorb all of this immediately. They'll need lots of reinforcement as you use commas in all of your model writing.

Below is an example of how students might record notes:

LINE	REASON FOR COMMA
1	after the day in a date
2	after the greeting (salutation) in a friendly letter
3	before conjunctions in compound sentences
7	around appositives that rename (opening comma)*
7	around appositives (closing comma)
7	separate prepositional phrases between the subject and verb (open)
7	separate prepositional phrases between the subject and verb (close)
8	after introductory phrases and clauses before the subject
9	to set apart descriptive phrases
14	to set apart descriptive phrases (participial)
15	to set apart the name of someone being addressed
19	before conjunctions in compound sentences
19	after introductory phrases and clauses
19	before conjunctions in compound sentences
21	after a letter closing

You may wish to mention that it is acceptable not to place commas around appositives that are only one word.

6. Have students place their lists in their writing folders for future reference.

5. You may want to read back over your piece asking students to notice how the commas affect your phrasing—they are "read" as brief pauses.

Coming to America: Ellis Island

Days 20 and Beyond: Creating a Readers Theater Script— We Are America

1. By this point, students have amassed a great deal of knowledge— through research, quotations, interviews, Read Alouds, independent reading, and journaling—about the immigrants who came through Ellis Island at the turn of the twentieth century. We culminate this unit with a dramatic Readers Theater that calls upon all the information your students have gathered and written. Students should recognize the framework of the drama as the words from the Statue of Liberty.

2. Students work with cooperative groups on various stages of the development of this dramatic reading. Organize the class into four to five cooperative groups. Every group is responsible for finding five excerpt samples from their research, journals, books, interviews, etc. The samples are as follows:

   Sample 1: An excerpt that tells why an immigrant(s) wanted to come to America. Include the name of the country from which they are emigrating.

   Sample 2: An excerpt from a personal account of the turbulent journey to America.

   Sample 3: An excerpt from an account of an immigrant's first sighting of the Statue of Liberty.

   Sample 4: An excerpt from an experience on Ellis Island as immigrants are examined.

   Sample 5: An excerpt from a newly declared American citizen.

3. Designate groups with a number and give each group a task card that defines their task as follows:

   Group 1: Collect all five required excerpt samples from each group (including their own). Organize the excerpts so that they'll be easy to review. Pass these to Group 2.

   Group 2: Review all submitted excerpts and choose the best for this production. Consider a mixture of short and longer pieces that best represent the category.

   Group 3: Insert the excerpts in the framework in the spots indicated, and then type and edit the text. (Can recruit help for typing from other group members, especially from Group 1.)

   Group 4: Cast and assign the readers to their parts, using all students in the production. Decide on expression and intonation of readers.

   Group 5 (optional): Technology component—Produce video clips or images on overhead projector to add dimension to the dramatic reading.

4. Using a transparency, present the rubric on page 88 to the class. This rubric describes how you will evaluate their production.

> **Language arts standard in this lesson:**
>
> Planning writing with details, using notes and logs, outlines, etc.
>
> Writing informational pieces (summarize and organize ideas gained from multiple sources in useful ways)
>
> Writing plays
>
> Editing for correctness, meaning, and clarity
>
> Using a simple checklist for revising and editing, working independently and collaboratively
>
> Publishing in various formats
>
> Using available technology for presentations

The excerpts chosen clearly met the defined requirements.	1 2 3 4
Revisions and editing of written pieces helped readers interpret and communicate the ideas.	1 2 3 4
First-person accounts demonstrated appropriate voice of the character, situation, and era.	1 2 3 4
Oral readings gave further meaning to the events by use of expression and intonation.	1 2 3 4
Technology creatively enhanced the drama.	1 2 3 4
Group 1 members collaborated and cooperated.	1 2 3 4
Group 2 members collaborated and cooperated.	1 2 3 4
Group 3 members collaborated and cooperated.	1 2 3 4
Group 4 members collaborated and cooperated.	1 2 3 4
Group 5 members collaborated and cooperated.	1 2 3 4
Total Points	____/40

(Divide 40 into the points earned to arrive at a numerical score if needed.)

5. Have students practice and present their Readers Theater performance for parents or other classes.

READERS THEATER SCRIPT FOR "WE ARE AMERICA"

Chorus: We are America.
(Insert three excerpts about why different people wanted to come to America. Name countries and reasons.)

Reader 1: Excerpt 1a

Reader 2: Excerpt 2a

Reader 3: Excerpt 3a

Chorus: Give us your tired, your poor, your huddled masses yearning to breathe free.
(Insert three excerpts from personal accounts of the journey to America.)

Reader 4: Excerpt 1b

Reader 5: Excerpt 2b

Reader 6: Excerpt 3b

Chorus: Give us the wretched refuse of your teeming shore.
(Insert three excerpts from immigrants' first sight of the Statue of Liberty.)

Reader 7: Excerpt 1c

Reader 8: Excerpt 2c

Reader 9: Excerpt 3c

Chorus: Send these, the homeless, tempest-tost to us.
(Insert three excerpts from trials and tribulations of experience on Ellis Island.)

Reader 10: Excerpt 1d

Reader 11: Excerpt 2d

Reader 12: Excerpt 3d

Chorus: I lift my lamp beside the golden door!
(*Insert three excerpts from newly declared American citizens.*)

Reader 13: Excerpt 1e

Reader 14: Excerpt 2e

Reader 15: Excerpt 3e

Reader 16: Give me your tired,

Reader 17: your poor,

Reader 18: your huddled masses

Reader 19: yearning to breathe free.

All: Give us your tired, your poor,
    your huddled masses yearning to breathe free.

Reader 20: Give me the wretched refuse

Reader 21: of your teeming shore.

Reader 22: Send these,

Reader 23: the homeless,

Reader 24: tempest-tost

All: to us.

Reader 25: I lift my lamp

Reader 26: beside the golden door!

Group 1: Give us your tired, your poor,

Group 2: your huddled masses yearning to breathe free.

Group 3: Give us the wretched refuse of your teeming shore.

Group 4: Send these, the homeless, tempest-tost

All: to us.

Female Reader: I lift my lamp beside the golden door!

All: We are America!

Alpha-Key Words Chart

A	B	C	D	E	F
G	H	**Alpha-Key Words**		I	J
K	L			M	N
O	P	Q	R	S	T
U	V	W	X	Y	Z

Writing Lessons for the Content Areas SCHOLASTIC TEACHING RESOURCES

5W's Organizer

Who:

BEGINNING →

Where:

When:

MIDDLE

What:

Why:

END →

Conclusion:

Persuasive Writing Flow Chart

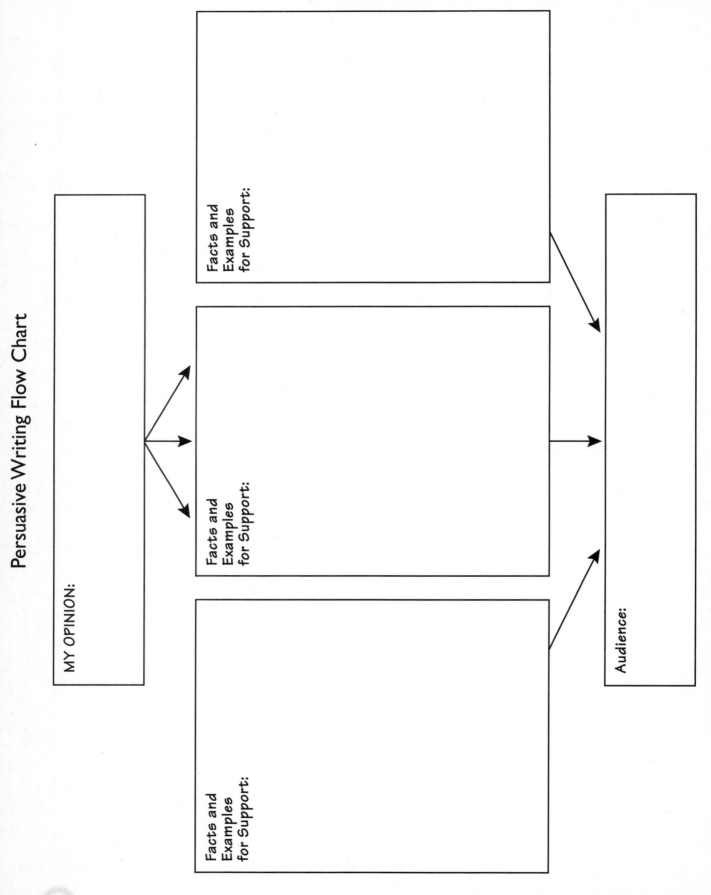

MY OPINION:

Facts and Examples for Support:

Facts and Examples for Support:

Facts and Examples for Support:

Audience:

Research Organizer

Front Side of Form

TOPIC: ______________________
____

Questions I have about this topic:

1

QUESTION 2: ______________________
____

Notes: ______________________

5

QUESTION 1: ______________________
____

Notes: ______________________

3

QUESTION 3: ______________________
____

Notes: ______________________

7

Back Side of Form

What I've learned about
Question 2:

6

(This page is blank.)

2

What I've learned about
Question 3:

8

What I've learned about
Question 1:

4

Note: For students' use, enlarge this form, make a two-sided master, and use this master for photocopies that students will cut apart and staple to create booklets.

Job Application

Name: _____

Position: _____

Qualifications: _____

_____

_____

_____

Previous Experience: _____

_____

_____

_____

References:

Name   Relationship

_____   _____

_____   _____

_____   _____

Previous Experience: _____

_____

_____

_____

_____

_____

Signature: _____   Date: _____

Research Report Organizer (One Source)

Topic: _____

_____

Title: _____

_____

_____

Resource: _____

Title: _____

Author: _____

Volume: _____   Pages: _____

_____

Question #1:

_____

_____

_____

_____

Question #2:

_____

_____

_____

_____

Question #3:

_____

_____

_____

_____

Bibliography

Bierman, Carol. *Journey to Ellis Island, How My Father Came to America*. New York: Hyperion Books for Children, 1998.

Bradby, Marie. *More Than Anything Else*. New York: Orchard, Scholastic Inc., 1995.

Charles, Robert. *Fossilized*. Bothell, WA: Wright Group/McGraw-Hill, 2002.

Cole, Judith Davis. *Better Answers*. Portland, ME: Stenhouse, 2002.

Copeland, Lamm and McKenna. *The World's Great Speeches, 4th edition*. New York: Dover Publishers, 1999.

Cramer, E. H. *Mental Imagery and Reading*. Bloomington, IL: Illinois Reading Council. 1992.

Dawson, Zoe. *Postcards from China*. Austin, TX: Steck-Vaughn Company, 1996.

Fredericks, Anthony D. *Animal Sharpshooters*. New York: Franklin Watts, A Division of Scholastic Inc., 1999.

Gambrell, L. B. and Koskinen, P. S. *Imagery: A Strategy for Enhancing Comprehension*. In C. C. Block and M. Pressley (Eds.), *Comprehension Instruction: Research-based Best Practices*. NY: Guilford Press, 2002.

Harvey, S. and Goudvis, A. *Strategies That Work: Teaching Comprehension to Enhance Understanding*. Portland, ME: Stenhouse, 2000.

Hesse, Karen. *Letters from Rifka*. New York: Puffin Books, 1992.

Hillocks, G., Jr. *Research on Written Composition: New Directions for Teaching*. Urbana, IL: National Conference on Research in English/ERIC Clearinghouse on Reading and Communication Skills, 1986.

Jacobs, William Jay. *Ellis Island New Hope in a New Land*. New York: Atheneum Books for Young Readers, 1990.

Keene, Ellin and Zimmermann, Susan. *Mosaic of Thought*. Portsmouth, NH: Heinemann, 1997.

Lasky, Katheryn. *Hope in My Heart, Sofia's Immigrant Diary, Book One: Sofia's Ellis Island Diary*. New York: Scholastic Inc., 2003.

Lawlor, Veronica, (Ed.). *I Was Dreaming to Come to America: Memories from Ellis Island Oral History Project*. New York: Puffin Books, 1997.

Leighton, Maxinne Rhea. *An Ellis Island Christmas*. New York: Puffin Books, 1994.

Levine, Ellen. *...If Your Name Was Changed at Ellis Island*. New York: Scholastic Inc., 1993.

Macarthur, B. *The Penguin Book of Twentieth Century Speeches*. Penguin USA, 2000.

Mariconda, Barbara. *Teaching Expository Writing*. New York: Scholastic Professional Books, 2001.

Mayberry, Jodine. *Business Leaders Who Built Financial Empires*. Austin, TX: Steck-Vaughn Company, 1994.

Moss, et al. "Exploring the Literature of Facts: Linking Reading and Writing Through Information Trade Books." *Language Arts*, Vol. 74, 1997.

Murray, Donald. 1984. Quoted in Alvermann, Phelps, *Content Reading Literacy*. Boston: Allyn & Bacon, 1998.

National Reading Panel. *Report of the National Reading Panel: Teaching Children to Read*. Washington, D.C.: National Institute of Child Health and Human Development, 2000.

Pikulski, John J. and Templeton, Shane. *Teaching and Developing Vocabulary: Key to Long-Term Reading Success*. Boston: Houghton Mifflin Company, 2004.

Stahl, S. A., and Fairbanks, M. M. "The Effects of Vocabulary Instruction: A Model-based Meta-analysis." *Review of Education Research*, 56(1), 1986.

Stein, Conrad R. *The California Gold Rush*. Chicago: Grolier Children's Press, 1995.

_____ *Teaching Content-Area Literacy Strategies*. Reading Essentials. Logan, Iowa: Perfection Learning Corporation, 2003.

Yolen, Jane. *Encounter*. New York: Viking Books, 1992.

Zemelman, S. et al. *Best Practice—New Standards for Teaching and Learning in America's Schools, 2nd Edition,* Portsmouth, NH: Heinemann, 1998.

Zinsser, William. *On Writing Well: The Classic Guide to Writing Non-Fiction*. New York: HarperResource, 2001.

Magazines Cited:

Appleseeds. A Cobblestone Publication, Carus Publishing Company.

Muse. Carus Publishing Company.

Ranger Rick. National Wildlife Federation

Sports Illustrated for Kids. The Time, Inc. Magazine Company

Time for Kids. The Time, Inc. Magazine Company

Web sites:

www.aei.ca/~star/mywebmaster.htm

www.americanrhetoric.com/speechbank.htm

www.ellisisland.org

www.enchantedlearning.com

www.historychannel.com/ellisisland

www.historychannel.com/speeches/

www.historyplace.com/speeches/previous.htm

www.howstuffworks.com

www.itrc.ucf.edu/conferences/fetc2004/images/writing.jpg

www.pbs.org/greatspeeches/timeline/

www.scholastic.com

www.surfnetkids.com/bookrpt.htm

www.teacher.scholastic.com/activities/immigration/tour

www.webmonkey.com